VIA Folios 128

CON AMORE

Bea Tusiani

CON AMORE

A Daughter-in-Law's Story of Growing Up
Italian American in Bushwick

Bea Tusiani

Bordighera Press

Library of Congress Control Number: 2017959263

First Edition © 2004

© 2017 by Bea Tusiani

All rights reserved. Parts of this book may be reprinted only by written permission from the author, and may not be reproduced for publication in book, magazine, or electronic media of any kind, except for purposes of literary review by critics.

Printed in the United States.

Published by
BORDIGHERA PRESS
John D. Calandra Italian American Institute
25 West 43rd Street, 17th Floor
New York, NY 10036

VIA FOLIOS 128
ISBN 978-1-59954-123-5

Dedicated to

Pamela Ann Tusiani

whose struggle in life
taught me to focus
on what is truly meaningful

Acknowlegements

Everyone who's reached a certain age, and has had time to reflect, knows the story of our past isn't always remembered the way it happened. I'm sure the family, friends and colleagues I write about in this memoir would tell their stories differently and I would love to have the opportunity some day to read them

Until such time, I wish to acknowledge the grace with which my family members reacted to their portrayals in this book. My two aunts, Bea and Minnie, my children Michael and Paula, and their spouses, Catherine and Roger were particularly helpful in providing feedback in their individual reviews. My husband Michael deserves much credit for allowing me total and absolute freedom to invade his privacy (which he holds above all else, most dear) as does his incomparable brother Joseph, who painstakingly sat by my side to scour each draft for possible inaccuracies and redundancies.

But this book would never have been written were it not for Lou Stanek and her memoir-writing class at the New School. Lou's encouragement there, and subsequently, in private work shop she ran, inspired me to release the stories pent-up in me for over 50-plus years. Helping to shape those stories into this book were fellow writers Jennifer Huntley, Gerry Cornez, Barbara Klaus, Susan Onaitis, Judith Zabar, and Fran Epstein. My writing muse, children's book author Eve Feldman, served as the angel-on-my shoulder throughout this process.

Lastly, I wish to send a special message to the incredible lady who's vast influence over me became the backbone of this life saga. "Con Amore, ma, con amore!"

Table of Contents

Introduction (1)

Part I – "BeBe" Stories (5)

1. Uncommon Name
2. Bang the Pipe Loudly
3. It Was a Jungle Out There
4. Entering a Brave New World
5. Grove Street 1950's
6. Weekends Abroad
7. Across the Street & Up The Block
8. Puppy Love
9. Who's Sorry Now?
10. Holiday Shorts

Part II – Bubbles (57)

11. Slapping Bubbles
12. Gates Avenue Gang
13. Dancing in Our Seats
14. Fairy Godmother
15. Boys in My Hood
16. Beach Days
17. Chubette to Cha-Cha
18. Oh Bushwick, My Bushwick!
19. Collapse of the House of Cards

Part III – Beattie (99)

20. The Three Judges
21. Waiting in the Wings
22. Unto the Son

23. A Rose and Her Thorny Issues
24. A Christmas Legacy
25. The Three Bears

Part IV – Bice (129)

26. Big City Campus
27. Fairy Tales Do Come True
28. The Heart
29. Reading, Writing and Room 308
30. When Daddy and I Got Married
31. Madonna of the Pot
32. Great Expectations
33. A Tale of Two Puppies
34. Just Between Us
35. Bad Vibes
36. *Bred, Sepalee & Pitza*
37. Mother Writer
38. Gastronomic Mania
39. Catastrophe
40. Saving Face
41. Don't Call Me Carmela
42. Crystal Ball
43. Mamma Mia, Maria

Epilogue – Mom's Letter (213)

Postscript (215)

INTRODUCTION

It may have been pure coincidence, but after four fainting spells, a subdural hematoma, and a life-threatening craniotomy, my old-fashioned, ninety-two year old Italian-born mother-in-law loudly proclaimed to anyone at the nursing home where she spent the last years of her life, her baby boy and I had married for love.

"Maichino e Beatrice si sono sposati con amore," she gushed with uncharacteristic enthusiasm. It didn't matter that my 5-foot, 115 lb. frail mother of all mothers-in-law made this pronouncement at a time in her life when hardly anything else she said made much sense, I craved her acceptance any way I could get it. "Con amore, con amore," trumpets rang in my ears and my eyes turned drippy at the music in her voice – finally, she was admitting Mike and I were a good match.

Arriving at that point wasn't easy. Gaining her favor was a challenge from the very first day my steady boyfriend told his mother he was dating "una siciliana." A chair and glass of water calmed her initially, but the indomitable matriarch insisted on seeing a map of Italy to pinpoint exactly where my hometown was on this reputed island of ruffians, in relation to the mainland of her own well-bred Apulian ancestors. From then on, it was my struggle to convince this tiny lady who turned out to be the biggest influence in my life, that even as a second generation American, I was still Italian enough to mix with her son's more rarified first-generation strain.

For more than twenty-five years our mother-in-law/daughter-in-law relationship grew into a parallel test of wills distanced by cultural and intergenerational gaps as wide as the ocean that separated the old country from the new. Time and again my modern American vices were pitted against her old-fashioned virtues. If I tossed a lone piece of string into the garbage, she'd catch it mid-flight and use it to tie up her tomato plants. "Quanto costa?" she asked when a melon she ate was particularly sweet. I learned to lie about such things because there was no doubt in both our minds that I spent more than I should have.

My Italian "suocera" dismissed most anything I did with a backward wave of the hand. Whether it was making meatballs, sewing a button on a shirt or treating a child's sore throat, my immaturity was always up against the wealth of experience culled from her hardscrabble life. So it was only natural for me to look over my shoulder one day when I heard her tell the aides behind the nurses' station, "questa è mia figlia," (this is my daughter). When I realized she was referring to me, I melted into a puddle.

I don't know why it took so long for my mother-in-law to acknowledge me so tenderly. I was loyal, respectful and loved her son and his family deeply. Having kept strong ties to both the land of my ancestors and the Bushwick community in Brooklyn where I was raised, I cared about my heritage and upbringing just as much as she did hers. Yet, whenever I tried to impart some small thread of the fabric of how I came to be who I am, it was never taken quite as seriously as the fiercely protected sphere of her own family's ties to Italy and the Bronx.

It was my lot, I figured, to remain a satellite in my mother-in-law's insular world. So I listened, with a healthy dose of respect and feigned interest to the same tales repeated over and over again. By heart, I knew Maria Pisone's father died the day she was born, that she finished school after third grade and went on to teach sewing classes to other young girls in the little hamlet of San Marco in Lamis. I suffered too, through long narrations of the profound sacrifices she made, raising my brother-in-law single-handedly while her husband of a mere three months went off to America; of how hard she worked, ironing and making shirts for wealthy landowners to put her only son through school, and how it paid off for him with an excellent education and some savings that allowed mother and son to make the journey twenty-three years later, to rejoin a long-lost husband and father they barely knew. And, climactically, how the unplanned birth of my American-born husband was received with a mixture of joy and shame for the quarter-century difference in age between the two brothers.

The aproned "donna di casa" repeated this highly prized family lore, mostly on Sunday afternoons after dinner as we two women of the household cleared the kitchen table and washed the dishes in her provincial ground floor apartment, while the men napped on the sofa or listened to opera. By the time the last spoon was dried and put away, I'd heard yet another rendition of how the midwife delivered my husband to the cheers of neighborhood paesani.

"Maichino era un bambino bello," little Michael was a beautiful baby, she managed to say with the same level of fervor undiminished by time. I loved my husband, but with each successive telling of how he spurned his mother's breast milk or fell off a bike and knocked out his two front teeth, I was beginning to resent him.

Jealousy? Sure. Compared to his rich personal history, I felt like an abandoned child. There was no one in my family to recount the important events of my life. My mother died when I was twenty-one, so long ago that I can hardly remember her voice, though I see her face every time I look in the mirror. My dad, who lived well into his eighties, didn't speak Italian, and even if he could, was too self-involved to sit around with my mother-in-law and chat about me. More than anything, I began to feel the need to hold onto my own memories if only to prove that I, too, have a past from which to draw my own historical beginnings, and it does matter in other peoples' worlds.

"Maria Bella," as my mother-in-law was referred to by the doctor who cared for her in her last years, died hours shy of her 95th birthday. A lofty milestone—"novantacinque anni"—another story, I'm sure, she would have proudly added to her repertoire.

But she never will. It's my story now. Or, her final story conveyed through me. Maybe she realized it would happen that way, and passed the torch to me, by revealing her emotional underpinnings in the increasing vocal chants that I had married her son "con amore." In the end, she may have sensed that I was the only "figlia mia" she'd ever have.

She taught me a lot—how to speak Italian, eat figs, make bread, crochet, and I taught her some things too, like how to make a meal without pasta, and that children can actually ride bikes without breaking their teeth. But while there was so much of my mother-in-law in my life, there was so little of mine in hers.

Had I been able to capture her full and absolute attention for one whole day, conversing fluently with her in English, I would have filled Maria Bella's head with stories of my own. Heaven only knows what she would have thought of BeBe.

PART 1 - BEBE STORIES

Il proverbio: "è una ruota che gira" — a wheel always makes a complete turn.

My mother-in-law never knew the sixteen cousins I had on my father's side of the family. Most of us grew up together during the 1940s and '50s a few blocks east and west of each other in our Bushwick, Brooklyn neighborhood. I was the second youngest grandchild born into the pure-bred Sicilian clan of Rose and Vito Cicio, and that was the reason, I always thought my aunts, uncles and particularly my cousins pinched my cheeks and called me "little BeBe."

Sixty years later, as I exit the prime of a baby-boomer's midlife, they still ask for Cousin "BeBe" when they call on the telephone and I get giddy every time I hear it. Despite my graying temples and sagging chin, that's who I'll always be.

It's not that I hadn't been called by other names growing up. My mother's side of the family, also pure-bred Sicilians, the LaSallas, had their own colorful way of getting my attention. "Spoiled brat," was Aunt Bea's favorite, and Uncle Joe's was "fatty pants." Aunt Minnie called me "rotten kid," and my sister, "snot nose." Even my father (traitor as he was to his side of the family) labeled me "chubby cheeks," and in his usual colorful wisecracking way, he wasn't referring to my face.

My mother was the only one who consistently called me my given name — Beatrice — and that's how my husband has always referred to me in the forty-six years we've been married. Until recently, that is. I've begun to hear a playful, totally unexpected but welcome "BeBe" slip out of his normally staid mouth. Perhaps he's discovered what my throng of cousins knew all along.

AN UNCOMMON NAME

Maria Bella had no idea what it was like to be christened "Beatrice."

"Why didn't you name me Patricia?" I asked my mother time and again when I was young. I wanted the more normal name of my best friend and all the attributes that went along with it—long curly blond hair, a graceful lithe body and dimpled smile. Instead, I was squat, dark and clumsy—what anyone would picture a Beatrice to be. I hated the way I looked and was sure that my name had everything to do with it.

Clearly, I was a victim of tradition. Born into a family with southern Italian roots, I knew that it was considered a sign of respect to name one's offspring after both sets of grandparents. My brother and sister turned out to be luckier in the line of succession. Born the first boy and girl, they were named after my father's parents, Rose and Vito.

Though that too, turned out to be problem in a large family such as mine, since all of my girl cousins were named some variation of Rose—Rosemarie, Rosalie. As for the boys, for some inexplicable reason, six of them originally named Vito later changed their names to William. But, while the Willies and Rosies in my family could at least commiserate with each other about their common fate, I was destined to stand alone.

As the third child born to Ignatius and Leonarda Cicio, my mother's mother's name, Beatrice, was handed down to me. Since my mom's sister never gave birth to more than two children, I was the only child branded with this solitary imprint.

Not only was I the only Beatrice among my cousins, but not a single one of my friends or classmates, nor anyone else in my entire Brooklyn neighborhood was named Beatrice. Cries of "B-B-gun" and "B-B-eyes" taunted me throughout my youth. Once I learned to read, I soon realized that there were more barnyard animals, most notably hens and cows, named Beatrice than there were human beings.

I'm quite sure that being a "Beatrice" in high school automatically classified me as a serious student. After all, how many cheerleaders or prom queens were named Beatrice? My teachers didn't help any, they'd always pause while taking attendance to emphasize the pronunciation of my name: "BEEch-riss" and the killer "Be-AH-triss" always made me slide deeper into my seat. No Linda or Cathy ever knew the silent impact of their ordinary names.

It wasn't until college, where some of my fellow classmates' names — Dimitri, Sharnaz, Concepcion — made mine less noticeable, but it did continue to torment me in unexpected ways. Upon introducing myself to a blind-date, he duly informed me that there was a town in Nebraska named "Be-YAT-riss."

In time, my literary pursuits led me to Dante, where I quite readily found my niche, preferring to become more closely associated with the legendary Beatrice Portinari of thirteenth century Florence, whose beauty was the inspiration for the poet's "Divine Comedy." Quite incidentally, or perhaps through another kind of fate, Dante turned out to be the middle name of the man with whom I eventually fell in love. For the first time in my life, I did not fight the interpretation of my name, but instead, used it coyly to my advantage.

I married my Dante and, with time, the silent resentment I bore against the antiquated ritual that made me glaringly different from everyone else, seemed to dissipate. It wasn't until my grandmother died forty years ago, I realized our name was just one small part of what we shared.

Barreling down the dark oak-scented stairway from the top floor of our three family house, I'd fling open the door to Gram's ground floor kitchen and sit on her full-skirted rocker from which vantage point I'd observe the family matriarch perform her daily tasks. I watched how she'd lift a white shirt with a wooden spoon from a boiling pan of bleach and water and deposit it on an enamel drain board, then follow her movement over to a steamer-trunk where she'd stored a week's worth of hard bread and grate it into breadcrumbs on top of a splayed paper bag.

Grandma Beatrice owned one of the few books in our whole three-story house—it was about Italy. As I watched her move about the kitchen, from stove, to sink, to table, I'd flip the pages of this treasured book and talk to her about the pictures and maps inside. She didn't know much about anything other than her own hometown of Santa Margherita Belice in Sicily where she lived until she was sixteen years old, but that proved to be enough of a catalyst to generate lively discussions between us. She relayed stories about the abundant cacti that sprouted prickly pears in her hometown and I lectured her about industrialized Milan and Genoa's busy seaport, and at some point during those very elementary sessions, she imparted to me, and I absorbed, a love for her homeland.

"Dalla che bella, dalla che bella, la lupa suona, pecora balla!" was a song she'd remembered singing when she was a young child living on a farm. She vividly recalled how on her daily trips to the fields to bring her father his lunch, she'd sing this song while stopping for a drink at a particular water spigot along the way.

I picked up other facets of our culture while helping her bake traditional Christmas cookies: fig-filled "cuccitate," "cassadate" filled with ricotta and the finger-licking honey dipped pignolate. She taught me to play popular Italian cardgames—scopa and briscola—how to plant basil and then mix it with eggs, parmesan cheese and bread to make 'pane con uova e basilico' for a summer breakfast when the herb was plentiful.

The seeds of family lore that my grandmother planted in me were destined to take root. I knew at some point in my life I would go back to Sicily to walk the streets, feel the earth, smell the air. When I finally did, I searched for and found the small water spout that she drank from, and as if performing some ancient ceremonial rite, bent down and drank from it as I imagined she once did. And standing on farmland that belonged to a great-grandfather I never knew, I was keenly aware that his genes were somehow reflected in me as I stood upon on his humble earth.

Since then, the tug and pull of tradition has made me understand why names such as mine were passed along from generation to generation, if only to question their significance in a time and place that were different from today's. But, having made it a point to name my two daughters the American homogenized names of Paula and Pamela, I recognize that I have cut the chain. There will be no more Beatrices linking my family's past with future generations, and the triumph of accomplishing that has turned out to be bittersweet.

BANG THE PIPE LOUDLY

When Mike and I were engaged, my mother-in-law offered to buy a two family- house for all of us to live in together. Having grown up under the watchful eyes of a houseful of relatives, I had my reservations.

The hallway in my grandmother's three story walk up was a communal living space where the eleven of us who lived there, had a looking glass into each other's lives. Gram, a widow since I was four, lived with my spinster Aunt Minnie in three of the most spacious rooms on the first floor. Aunt Bea occupied four rooms on the second floor with her perfect family of four: Uncle Joe, my younger cousin and perennial cohort Joseph, and the much fussed-over baby

Geraldine. We didn't know it then, but my mom, dad, older brother and sister and I had the penthouse—five railroad rooms strung tightly together with no privacy—on the top floor.

Aside from the shared hallway and stairwells, the only other building feature that connected my mother's apartment with her two sisters' was the cylindrical hot water pipe that snaked through each ceiling and floor.

"Go bang the pipe," my mother said when she had something to convey to one of her sisters or mother. Accustomed to what at the time seemed like a normal request, I'd walk over to the kitchen drawer, take out a heavy butter knife, walk back into the dining room and send a resouding message of tappity-tap-taps that trickled down to the two apartments below. My mother would then open the kitchen window and swing her head out. Craning their heads up from their own windows down below were two similar figures asking why she had banged.

"The LaMarca's are coming over for coffee, do you have any cake?" it might be this time. Another time, Aunt Bea would bang on the pipe because she needed help taking the carriage out, or Aunt Min banged to tell someone upstairs there was a phone call.

In those days, the early 1950's, there was only one telephone for all three of our families, and we were considered lucky because most of our neighbors still had to go around the corner to Barbara Ann's Candy Store to make and receive calls on a pay phone. Ours was a heavy black rotary device with thick fabric cord and true bell-tone ring that was treated with utmost respect since its use signaled a matter of extreme importance. Using it to call a doctor if someone was sick, or receiving long-distance calls from my brother when he was in the Air Force stationed in Korea were allowed, but chatty calls to a neighbor or, God-forbid, one from my sister's boyfriend, were not.

The phone sat on a large oak chest of drawers yellowed with time. Attached to the chest was a swinging mirror with aged black spots marring its reflection. I liked it best when Gram lit a votive candle on the anniversary or birthday of some poor dear-departed soul, and all day the flame would flicker in two places, the red glass cup in which it sat, and its scratchy mirror image. A chipped but very regal- looking statue of the Infant of Prague stood as the candle's recipient, patiently absorbing its prayerful intention. Ever curious, my cousin Joseph and I always checked inside the drawers of "the bureau" as it was familiarly referred to, and dipping our hands deep into its recesses, often recoiled with splinters hiding in the wood.

Then we'd knock on Gram's door and while admonishing us for putting our hands where they didn't belong, she'd take us into her bathroom to find alcohol and a tweezer to remove the pesky sliver. Unlike the two hall bathrooms upstairs, Gram's ground floor bathroom was as frigid as a walk-in freezer. Situated closest to the backyard, it was unheated. Blasts of wintry wind whistled through its rickety window. I never dawdled when I went to the toilet in Gram's house because I feared my tender bottom would freeze and I'd be stuck to the seat.

Exiting the bathroom, past the bureau and Gram's kitchen door, in the center of the downstairs hall were two staircases: one dark and dank smelling led to the basement, the other fragrant with furniture polish rose to the second floor.

Beyond the stairs was the front door, which served as the main entrance for everyone who lived in the house; next to it stood the bin. Dug deeply into the cement under the front stoop, the hovel-like bin held folding chairs, shovels, umbrellas, extra rope for snapped clotheslines and everyone's thick rubber galoshes (the adults' were black, Joseph's and mine, red.)

One day I was summoned, via banging on the pipe, down to the first floor by my mother, who along with the rest of the family members, visited Gram in her apartment off and on throughout the day.

"What?" I asked from the window, dragging my lazy bones away from under the dining room table where I'd propped my head against its legs to watch our new 12" Motorola television set.

"Come down here right away," she said in a tone I knew only too well signaled I was in trouble.

The three judges were waiting for me at the bottom of the first-floor landing with folded arms. I hung back a few steps before the onslaught hit. My mother, flanked by her two sisters, grabbed hold of my arm and marched me into the bin where big white letters scrawled FUCK!

Puzzled, I looked blankly back at them. The torrent of accusations burned holes in my ears.

"I didn't do it," I cried over and over again as I was being pulled away by my elbow. But no one believed me.

"You should be ashamed of yourself," screeched Aunt Bea in her holier than thou voice. "I don't want my Joseph to pick up these bad habits from your daughter," she said haughtily to my mother who, in turn, squeezed her eyes at me.

My father, my Uncle Joe — not even the men, believed me. I was officially labeled "a bad influence," and shunned by most of the adults (my parents didn't dare tell Gram about it for fear she'd scold them for raising such a bad kid). After my punishment of going to my room expired, I went looking for my cousin Joseph, and, sure enough, the smirk on his face told me all I needed to know.

"Oh you," said Aunt Bea when I knocked on her door trying to reclaim my reputation. "You're always trying to put the blame on someone else." I was so frustrated I was tempted to empty the can of Johnson's Baby Powder into Geraldine's cherished buggy.

I felt the same way the time my sister didn't believe I'd written a poem while sitting on the top step of the third floor landing — a place that served as my first desk. Eager to share it with someone, I read it to the first person who came along — my sister — as she swished up the stairs in her gray poodle skirt.

"You copied that from a book," she sneered. Once again, I was unable to defend myself. That night, I prayed with all my might the long mirror in the second floor vestibule would crack the next time my sister pranced in front of it, to flare her crinolines.

"Mirror, mirror on the wall, who's the fairest of them all? You're not," I fantasized the vile witch from Snow White responding to my evil sister.

Joseph and I always played in that vestibule on rainy and snowy days, or when others couldn't be bothered to watch us and we were considered "safe" inside the house. Skipping back and forth from the vestibule, back to a big, wide step that cut the third floor stairwell in half, we'd slide down the banister, shoot our fake guns through its railings and drape blankets over its turreted posts in our madcap portrayals of cowboys and Indians, cops and robbers, Tarzan and Jane.

Only my family members were inconvenienced, since they were the ones who had to step over our canteens and makeshift tents in order to reach the third floor. When I was older and it was quiet, I did a lot of writing on the top step of that third floor landing. But often it bustled with activity. The bathroom was at one end, and a small open storage closet that held a ladder and the ironing board was at the other. Once-a-year Grandma and Aunt Bea would make a pilgrimage to the third floor landing (Aunt Min, being single, worked) where they joined my mother in stretching out all the handmade family heirlooms on drying racks studded with protruding nails.

They assembled these table-sized rectangular frames on the top floor where there'd be less traffic to mar the finely crocheted tablecloths, drapes and antimacassars that graced all the furniture (including Gram's refrigerator and the downstairs' bureau), after they'd been bleached and starched and pulled-tight while wet to prevent shrinkage.

Joseph and I were never allowed to go near the racks when something was being stretched, but in between dryings, we were fascinated by the nails and played a game to see how deeply they would go into our skin before piercing through. Had our mothers ever discovered the blood on the nails where they hung their pristine white heirlooms Joseph and I surely would have been crucified together on those very racks!

The third floor hall bathroom was another bane of my existence. I was afraid to use it ever since my sister came running through the apartment late one night after a date. With her pants down around her knees, she woke us all up — jumped on the double bed we shared, and screamed she'd seen a mouse run under the bathtub. My father set up a trap the next day, and although he was good at it — winning most of the daily pools for trapping mice in the cheese factory where he worked — it took a long time before he was able to catch this little Mickey.

I never went into the bathroom without slippers after this mousecapade and didn't sit long on the toilet either, because I was afraid the mouse my father finally caught and flushed would pop up and bite my butt. Much as I dreaded the bathroom because of its scary features, like the dark, drafty airshaft that loomed menacingly and noisily when the wind howled behind a hinged window above the tub where I bathed, I couldn't escape it. It was my chore to clean the bathroom on Saturdays.

Doing so one day, I left my task briefly to search for my father out the window, eagerly anticipating his return with the hot dogs he always brought from the street-corner vendor two blocks away on Wilson Avenue after we'd all finished our shared chores every Saturday. Not two minutes passed before there was a commotion. I ran back to find the sink I'd been rinsing the cleanser out of had overflowed. Waves of water curled around the bathroom door and down the stairs. Apparently, it was leaking through the ceiling into Aunt Bea's bathroom too. Hah!

In the hallways of life, there is sweet justice.

IT WAS A JUNGLE OUT THERE

Unlike my mother-in-law who could make soup out of a wasp's nest if she had to, I could be victimized by an army of ants.

From the very second I climbed over the big cement step leading to the backyard of our three story house, I stalked and was hunted down by the scary beasts of Brooklyn's urban wildlife. Dragon flies (called dining-needles by the skallywags in my neighborhood), praying mantis, beetles, scorpions, black widow spiders and even alley cats, caused me to scream in loud blasting shrieks for my Grandma's attention and hopeful rescue.

She had the unenviable job of minding me and Joseph, who was two years younger than I, from her ground floor kitchen window while her daughters, our mothers, tended to housewifely duties upstairs in their second and third floor apartments. I was about five, and Joseph three, when we were first let out in the backyard to play every day in nice weather as a means of containing us, fenced-in and protected in an earthly playpen.

During those early years, my cousin and I innocently explored every inch of our 20x40 foot backyard. This adventureland was the Disney World of our childhood. Just beyond the back door and taking up the first-third of the area's rectangular shape was a cement surface that slanted slightly from all directions toward a sieve-like drain. This is where Joseph and I amused ourselves drawing with colored chalk, or, on unbearably hot days, splashed in a steady rain of water from a hose tied up to a pipe above our heads, or played ball. Gram would pass us our lunch from her kitchen window as well as drinks, spoons to dig with, a blanket, rope, clothespins and any other annoying thing we requested for our childish play. The only time she actually came out into the yard was when she sensed danger. Like the time Joseph and I made a big ruckus because a humongous black beetle flew into the yard and landed in front of our only escape route: the back door leading into the house.

Grandma peeked out, went back into the long narrow hallway and reappeared with a playing card. She placed the card over the plum-sized intruder and squashed it with her well-worn black laced tie-up. Lifting her foot, she took the card—I vividly remember it was a Queen of Spades—scooped up the beetle's sorry carcass and flipped its dead remains over the fence into Mrs. Lombardi's yard.

As we got older, Grandma became wiser and didn't respond to our every screech and holler. One time Joseph, whom everyone in the family thought of as genteel and sweet (except me, I knew better), taunted me that the black spider climbing up my pant leg was a deadly black widow. I wailed for help to no avail. I had reason to believe my cousin because he'd previously saved the two of us from an orange-colored creature we'd innocently found under a rock behind Grandpa Jack's jerry-built dog house—a scary place where we rarely ventured. It turned out to be a scorpion. Joseph identified it from a picture he'd seen in a book. I had no idea what a scorpion or black widow looked like, but Joseph seemed very sure of himself, so I figured it must be a boy-thing.

Some days Gram impishly engaged in our childish play. Whenever she bought snails, to make "babalugia," a Sicilian version of escargot, made with oil, garlic and mint, she always pulled a few of the slimy creatures off of her white enamel drainboard and placed them on her windowsill for us to play with. Divvying them up by size and color, Joseph and I raced them, stuck them on the bathroom window where they tracked long lines of wet goo and hid them in secret places. The postman jumped ten feet in the air one day when he found one in our mailbox.

My cousin and I never did take to eating the little buggers, though the old-timers just swooned from their succulence. The crabs my dad and Uncle Joe caught in Canarsie during the summer were more to our liking. We marveled at how basketfuls of the iridescent blue shellfish turned orangey-red after Grandma grabbed each one by its belly and slapped it down into a bubbling cauldron of boiling water. For a long time we actually thought she added some kind of dye to the pot—like the ones she used for Easter eggs—to change their color.

Like everyone else in the family, Joseph and I eagerly lined up for the platterfuls of crabs piled into mounds that were passed through Grandma's kitchen window into the yard where a wooden picnic table was spread with newspapers for the messy cracking and snapping involved in eating these wily creatures. I could put away half a dozen myself—though there was very little meat to make it a hearty meal; the joy was in biting down on and sucking the sweet juices from each slender claw. Joseph and I always hid some of the biggest claws in the metal box where Grandma planted basil, parsley and her very favorite herb, mint, and retrieved them the following day to play fishermen with the crab cages our fathers left out in yard the night before.

Perhaps the perennial smell of fish in our backyard drew the attention of Ginger, a stray cat Joseph claimed for our own. She sized us up, cautiously meandering on the outskirts of our intensive frolicking play, and seemed to want to join in. Gram wasn't pleased that we sat with Ginger at her kitchen window, badgering her for plates of milk and asking for a rope to put around the reluctant cat's neck so we could take her out front to parade her up and down the block. "I told you so," she admonished, when Joseph and I returned minutes later with only the rope. We never did see Ginger again, though we were always on the lookout for her.

Our escapades in the soil-covered garden section of the yard were equally adventuresome. Aside from Grandma's herb box and clinging red rose bushes, from which Joseph and I took frequent bouquets to our teachers, this part of the yard was infused with the spirit of our dead and unknown Grandpa Jack. A long cement path stretched under a grape arbor he had built with a criss-cross of iron poles that had long since rusted.

Fallen purple grapes scattered along the path drew armies of ants, a source of amusement for Joseph, but not so much for me as I feared them climbing into my underpants and socks. Oftentimes when we became engrossed in studying the work habits of these little creatures, following their progress from one grape to another, Grandma would come out with an enamel pot filled with hot water to wash the rotted fruit down the drain, drowning out whole artfully crafted anthills in the process.

Sometimes just after a heavy rainfall, we'd see larger, shell-less versions of our endearing snails in an uglier form — slugs. Joseph loved to prick them with twigs to watch their instinctive shyness pull away. During such a slugfest, to protect the tomato plants, my father would place a dish of beer out on the garden path to attract and drown the unwary creatures.

Just beyond some tomato plants tied along the fence was Grandpa's fig tree. Like Mr. Lombardi's fig tree, it was wrapped in tar paper and topped with a metal bucket to keep it warm in winter. Somewhere between the fig tree and the doghouse was the spot where Myrtle could usually be found. Joseph and I looked for the box turtle in this part of the yard at the beginning of every summer where it miraculously appeared like a blossoming bush, seemingly unearthed. We played with the turtle the way we did the slugs, prompting it to retreat from our prodding stones and twigs and leaves.

Beyond Myrtle's habitat stood the ominous and haunting dog house that Grandpa built to house his two trusty, long-gone pointers. He used them for hunting squirrels, rabbits and deer. Though Grandpa always gutted his catch in the basement, the tools of torture he used and remnants of skinned pelts, claws and skeletal carcasses still hung eerily from nails and hooks in this musky, enclosure. Joseph and I were both drawn to and repelled by with its menacing presence in our yard.

The same was true of the praying mantis that flew onto the house and wouldn't budge, disrupting our happy existence. Even Grandma knew that it was bad luck to kill a praying mantis, and that proved to be the turning point of our young lives. We couldn't count on her to get another card and step on the mammoth six-inch long insect. The threat of its constant presence put a crimp in our fanciful play until we no longer felt like the kings of our backyard jungle. Before long, we realized that adventures of a different kind awaited us in a new and different realm.

ENTERING A BRAVE NEW WORLD

I can't imagine a day in my mother-in-law's life filled with play.

When Joseph and I became bored playing with each other in the backyard, our parents gradually moved us to the front of the house where we could interact with other children in our closely-knit neighborhood. There, just beyond a latticed iron latch-key door was a gated square of cement that became home-base for my cousin and me throughout our early school years.

It was a struggle for the two of us to be patient, every summer morning waiting for Grandma to take up her post at a different window now, this one in her living room, where upon prior agreement with her two daughters, she kept us in her peripheral vision while she shelled peas or crocheted lace doilies for practically every piece of furniture in the house including the insides of the cupboards. Our perennial sergeant-at-arms, Grandma had to be more watchful when we played out front than she did when we were in the backyard because there was always the possibility we'd chase after something into the street. True to our childlike nature, we always did.

Up and down the city block there were similar shingled walk-ups and ruddy brownstones with front gates where children played by day and adults gathered on hot summer nights to drink beer and iced-tea on plastic-weaved folding chairs, basking in the last breezes of the day before going up to their sweaty beds. Our front gates provided a daily mecca for neighbors of all ages to commune and socialize, exchange news and gossip, and we clung to the familiarity of it as if we were one big extended family.

At first Joseph and I were limited to playing with tricycles, pull-toys, water-pistols and marbles. But peering between the rungs of the black wrought-iron fence out onto the brave new world up and down the sidewalk, we glimpsed what lay ahead as we grew older. Among our greatest thrills was hearing the oncoming clackety-clack of home-made scooters. Fashioned out of milk bottle crates, two-by-fours and the split halves of metal roller skates, these crudely made vehicles hit the gravel pavement with such clamorous force, we could hear their thunder half a block away. It wasn't speed that determined the value of these vehicles among the scooter brigade — because only on smooth slate surfaces could they go fast and anyone who ever roller-skated up and down Grove St. knew the sidewalks changed from bumpy to smooth in front of each house — but it was the number of sharp-toothed bottle caps hammered into their three sided hoods that drew the admiration of onlookers like my cousin and me.

I never had a milk-box scooter, but of course, Joseph did. It was almost a given since his dad was a milkman and good at carpentry. My dad was a shipping clerk in a cheese factory and used a hammer only as a weapon. But fortunately for me, just about the time we were allowed out of the front gate, the differences in our sexes came into play. While Joseph banged Rheingold and Piels beer caps onto his scooter with his new pals, Peter and Leonard, I became interested in playing girly games with Agatha from up the block and Roseann from down the block.

We girls hoarded bottle caps too, to play potsy, known as hopscotch in more delicate neighborhoods. These quarter-sized spheres were small enough to throw and land in one of the eight chalk-lined boxes in a rectangular grid, and easy enough to spot and grasp while hopping on one foot. Agatha used the discarded top of a tin can, folded into quarters, as her game-piece. I coveted her all-out technique for jettisoning her well-honed gold flying saucer into a numbered box and envied the way her sturdy laced up oxfords hit the pavement with a smart clap.

Whenever there were more than a few girls outside, we'd get together to jump rope.
"All, all, all in together girls
How do you like the weather girls?
Fine, fine."
Sometimes the boys moved in and convinced us to play High Water, Low Water by raising the jump rope like a limbo stick. Naturally, the boys were always better than the girls at this, though I don't know why, given the extra bit of anatomy that inevitably had to clear the rope.

Other games we played with the boys involved a streetlight as homebase. We'd shoot odd and even fingers into a circle to determine who was going to be "it." That person turned away from the pack of players who stood behind a starting line ready to advance. Leaning against the pole, whoever was "It" covered his eyes and shouted "Red light, green light, one, two, three" or "take 3 Giant Steps and two baby steps," before we could get past him, tag the pole and be "safe."

Any kid on the block who was lucky enough to own a Spaldeen had an automatic following. It meant we could choose up sides and play punchball. Our ballfield was concocted by making two manholes in the middle of the street, home and second base, and an opposing johnny pump and curbside sewer, first and third. Without the aid of a stick or bat, all punchball players needed was the battering whoosh of a tight fist and strong arm to send the pink ball spinning onto someone's front gate or stoop or down through a cellar door. A rooftop hit was an automatic home run and a smashed window signaled immediate retreat and sealed lips.

Less hazardous were the handball games played in pairs against the sides of houses that had no windows, or against a string of windowless garages. When it was just Joseph and me with a ball between us, we'd stake out two relatively even adjacent squares of sidewalk and play box-ball, by slapping a ball back and forth until one of us landed outside the other's box. If he wasn't around, I could still play a game of solitary stoop-ball, and try to hit valuable pointers bounced high off the sharp edge of a step.

Every afternoon around 4:30 my mother's embarrassing yell out the window, "Beatrice!" signaled it was time for me to go around the corner to Mr. Frank's grocery store where the Sicilian "scalida" bread had just been delivered fresh from LaRosa's Bakery. Standing under my third floor bedroom window with my mother overhead, I'd wait for the familiar brown paper wrapped package to sail down on me, twisted tight with exactly 14 cents. The one advantage of having to buy the bread every day was being able to get a head start on everyone else in the family eating it. Walking home, I'd pull off a crusty heel and savor it much the way the cowpokes on TV westerns bit into a tough piece of meat.

After dinner it was downstairs and out the door again. The biggest challenge I faced was how to spend the ten cents my father gave me every night. I could use it all up on one of the rides that stopped on our street. They all cost a dime. At first I had to accompany Joseph on the baby rides, lining up with the other neighborhood kids to quickly grab a horse or truck or fire engine and beep the horn or ring the bell. But as I grew older, I was eventually let out of that duty and looked forward to the jostling snap of the sharp-turning Whip or thrill of the rocking Half Moon as it gained momentum higher and higher into the screaming Brooklyn sky.

Soon I developed a plan. For three nights in a row I would spend 7 cents on a fudgicle bought from the Good Humor Man. On the fourth night, I'd have 9 cents saved up plus the dime my dad would give me. I could always scrounge up a penny to add to it and enjoy both a ride and fudgicle on the same night! Sometimes it worked, sometimes it didn't. When it didn't, I'd go to my uncle, two aunts or grandma with a sorrowful tale of woe. One time my sister made my life so much easier by spontaneously giving me a quarter—I just adored her after that.

If I was luckier still, some of my Cicio aunts and uncles would walk over from their homes on the surrounding blocks and visit with us in the front gate. I'd smile sweetly and let them pinch my cheek—Uncle Al was always good for a nickel—Uncle Joe actually gave me big shiny silver dollars but my mother never let me spend them. Having extra change in one's pocket always called for a trip around the corner to Barbara Ann's Candy store where a penny bought two Double Bubbles, or a Tootsie Roll, Chocolate Babies, a Red Hot or a stick of red or black licorice. Pretzel logs sold for 2 cents each; long strips of candy buttons a nickel and if you were flush, 7 cents bought a Creamsicle or pricey egg cream.

Walking back around the corner, young teens huddling together on stoops teased the way we younger ones sucked on our candy or mimicked our gait. My older sister and her stoop-group swatted me away as if I were an annoying mosquito, then turned back to the anguishing strains of Johnny Rae on a portable radio. Billowy scarves covered their hair set in pin-curls with bobby pins, tight blouses tucked into pedal-pushers—they preened for the leather-jacketed heartthrobs who gathered similarly on the opposite side of the street.

This age group stayed out the latest. We kids were sent up first, to bathe and get into our pajamas a good half hour before the adults started folding their chairs and emptying their bottles into the garbage cans. My mother thought I was in bed while she and my dad watched TV. They didn't know I'd steal over to my bedroom window one last time to peer out at the empty front gate.

GROVE STREET, 1950s

"Don't take your eyes off of them for a minute," my mother-in-law warned when her son and I broke the news that we were moving to the suburbs. She couldn't understand how I could let my children play outside by themselves.

It was hard for me to fathom. When I was growing up, a single city block in Bushwick was my entire world.

Every kid on Grove St. was afraid of running into Pork-Chop. Pork-Chop was the nick-name the neighborhood rascals pinned on the beefy dark-skinned janitor who tended to the four apartment buildings on the corner of Grove and Evergreen. He was big, and Frankenstein-like. Mostly, I remember the whites of his eyes.

It was common knowledge among us that Pork-Chop had a collection of little children's bones on the roof-top of one of his buildings. Because of this, whenever we ventured into the courtyards or connecting alleyways of the apartment complexes up the block, we'd always travel in pairs. Our biggest fear was that Pork-Chop was lurking behind the corner of some dark alleyway in search of a new skeleton to add to his pile of bones. Of course, we never really did see him do anything to children except chase us away, but that was terrifying enough, considering what we knew of him.

Scooting past the tall apartment buildings to escape Pork-Chop, we knew we were in safe territory when we reached the Tobacco Road houses. These two six-story buildings housed the poorest families of the block. Though no one was anything near rich on Grove Street (except for Mrs. Astor, but I'll get to her later) the people in the Tobacco Road houses seemed to be the poorest of us all.

These two dilapidated four-story buildings with rickety steps leading up to each splintered front door, and chips of tan-weathered paint crumbling from cellar doors, looked conspicuously different from the other, more respectable brick and shingled buildings on the block. Even the sidewalks in front of the Tobacco Road houses seemed to have more cracks than on any other part of Grove Street. The kids too, were different. There seemed to be dozens of them in each family, all with runny noses and tattered clothes. They sat on the fences, straddled the window frames and careened noisily in and out of the two narrow hallways. My mother always told me to stay away from the Tobacco Road children, they had lice in their hair, she warned. So I would walk quickly past these dwellings too. Mercifully, peace awaited me at the shrine.

The shrine was actually a big garage that housed the Church's statue of the Blessed Mother. Once a year in August, on the feast of the Assumption, this statue was carried out of the shrine on the shoulders of the neighborhood men and marched through the local streets. A procession would invariably form behind the holy statue and follow it back to the garage where it remained until the following year. This garage was set into the block at the end of a long, wide driveway — an unusual feature in Brooklyn in the 1950's. We children seized the opportunity to take advantage of the long paved driveway and the smooth garage doors at the end of it, which were perfect for playing handball. Though a sign above the garage, block-lettered in white, warned "no ball-playing," we were sure that the blessed statue inside would forgive us.

How, after all, can a child on a city-block resist a smooth wall when she has only a ball to play with? There is just so much stoop-ball, box-ball and punch-ball one can play before the need to smash a ball against something solid takes hold. Our instinctive youthful transgressions were usually short-lived because the old lady who lived above the garage would inevitably stick her head out the window. She'd point at us with her crooked index finger and swear that someday the saint in the garage would take vengeance on our ball-playing souls.

Fleeing the old lady, we'd hop over Jenny's front gate and hide behind the bushes, which served as a natural cover for our pre-adolescent bodies. We could always count on Jenny to protect us, because even though she was fifty she was just like us. "A little slow" was how my mother put it — her way of saying Jenny was retarded. But we kids accepted her as one of our own. Jenny's favorite pastime was watching us street urchins play. Many times I detected a glint in her eyes, as if she wanted to come out from behind her gate and play "red-light, green-light," or "giant-steps" with us. But she always remained on safe ground, in the small territory that fate dealt her.

Often while playing one of these street games, everyone would come to a complete standstill when 'Carmen Miranda' walked by. Carmen Miranda, another name the origin of which sprung from the neighborhood households and stuck forever. She mesmerized us. This tall, elegant woman lived in one of Pork-Chop's buildings up the block and every day around five o'clock she'd walk down Grove Street to go to work. We kids were not supposed to know her place of business was a strip-tease parlor under the Myrtle Avenue El.

Everyone, even the adults and especially the men, always stopped and stared when Carmen Miranda sauntered by. She'd always stare past us, keeping her black-turbaned head straight, dangling earrings swaying with every step of her spike-heeled shoes. She was the closest thing to a movie star that the people on Grove Street had ever seen.

Sometimes we'd whistle and make cat-calls at her, usually after she'd already passed by. It seemed harmless enough, as she never acknowledged our presence. One day though, I over-stepped my bounds. Letting out a long, low, very suggestive wolf-whistle while hiding behind a thick cast-iron lamp-post, I was suddenly smashed with an open-handed blow from behind. It was my mother — making such a commotion that Carmen Miranda turned around as well as my friends and the window-gapers high above. My mother's face colored beet-red, I guess I really embarrassed her, except that I'm sure Carmen didn't know who I belonged to before this unfortunate little incident occurred.

When I was finally allowed out of the house again, I went four doors away to my friend Roseann's. I loved Roseann but I hated her house — that is, ever since the drunk fell into the sewer there. The basement in Roseann's six-family walk-up had huge holes cut into its cement floor under which sewer water ran. Every time we wanted to play in Roseann's backyard, we had to pass through the basement, side-stepping these treacherous manhole-like pits to reach the steps and cellar door that led up to her yard.

Late one summer night someone discovered that the drunken man who notoriously roamed through the hallways of that house in a stupor, had fallen into one of these pits. I remember standing by the ambulance as the police carried the body bags out of Roseann's basement — one with an arm, another with some other piece of the wretched man's decomposed body.

I didn't go inside Roseann's house much after that grisly incident, mostly, we played on her stoop. It wasn't long before I became intrigued by the man that lived next door to her. He had a wooden leg, from a war injury, explained my mother. Every time "peg-leg" walked down the street, the neighborhood urchins would follow to see if they could catch a glimpse of wood. No one ever did, even though one of his legs was very stiff and the material of his pants hung loosely down that side. We even watched him go up the steps. . . still, no wood. All he really had to do was show it to us just once, and we probably would have left him alone, but he didn't, so we continued to badger him with our parade-like presence whenever he stepped out the door.

Just beyond 'peg-leg's' house were a string of garages;

one housed a gleaming Model-T Ford owned by a widow and her two bachelor brothers. The threesome took the shiny car out once a week to go to St. Barbara's Church, which was only two blocks away, and returned it to the garage to be enshrined like the saint until the following Sunday.

Across the street from these garages was the corner grocery. Its owner had a large collection of rifles and shotguns which he kept in his apartment above the store. I know this because I was in his daughter's class and I used to call for her from time to time. Her father was a quiet, good-natured man and I don't ever recall seeing a gun in his store, but every fourth of July while other city blocks were popping-off harmless little fireworks, our Mr. Groceryman would go up on his roof and blast round after resounding round of ammunition into the sky. No one ever dared filch even a small piece of bubble gum from *his* store.

Of all the people on the block Mrs. Astor was one who was set apart from the rest of us. Hers was the dream house we all longed to live in. It was a rare one-family cottage surrounded by a fence and actual grass. The only one of its kind on Grove Street, it represented the ultimate in luxury to us all: it even had a porch. I never learned much else about Mrs. Astor but her name. "Who do you think you are? Mrs. Astor?" was frequently invoked by the people on our block.

Spying all of these characters and street-scenes from above were anonymous window watchers who rarely went out. Mostly older people, they leaned their elbows on windowsill pillows dozens of times throughout the day. They knew everything about everybody on the street, but no one knew much about them. They were not the actors in this sometimes tragic or comic setting, but served as its audience, clapping and booing our performances day after day.

So many characters on one single city block. There were still more: the gray haired lady who had a change-of-life baby; Drunken Mary with dozens of cats spewing out of her haunted house; Arnold the giant and Alice the dwarf.

My own children would never know such people. They missed out on a lot growing up in the suburbs in an environment where Mrs. Astor's houses were the norm and the neighbors were virtual clones of one another. On hot summer days when they complained there was nothing to do... I knew how different it could have been.

WEEKENDS ABROAD

My mother-in-law's idea of a bathing suit was tucking her housedress up between her knees. I can only imagine what she thought when she saw me for the first time in my fully exposed red spandex number. She had no inkling I'd been weaned on them.

I'd just risen to the top of a see-saw when a herd of my relatives came running toward me in a wave of commotion. My stunned playmate sent me crashing to the ground. I was stunned too at the dragnet of aunts, cousins and siblings who apparently turned around to retrieve me once they realized I was missing from a caravan of family cars that had already departed from Casino Pool in Freeport, Long Island.

Being an eight-year-old involved the intricacies of childish play, I didn't notice that my relatives, clearly one-forth of the pool's weekend population, had packed up and taken off for the journey back to their Brooklyn neighborhoods. I couldn't tell by their mixed reactions whether they were happy or annoyed; hugs and kisses indicated they were grateful I wasn't lying at the bottom of the pool, and wagging fingers scolded me for not paying attention.

I guess they were right about my not paying attention. Having spent summers at Casino Pool since I was born, I should have known the pattern of comings and goings for our weekend treks abroad. The newly paved Southern State

Parkway was our link to places far away from the blisteringly hot sidewalks of New York City's streets. My dad and his brothers discovered this yellow brick road leading out to the country on their daily truck routes delivering butter and cheese to stores in the newly emerging suburbs.

Traveling *en masse* — my father's six siblings and my mother's two, with their spouses and pack of 18 kids — drove out to Freeport on weekends in the summer, or picnicked at Valley Stream State Park through the spring and fall during the 1940's and 50's. With every wedding and new baby born, the circle of in-laws, godparents and second cousins grew exponentially into a tribe, prompting us to devise a system whereby a few select members were sent out in advance to stake out tables and bar-b-que grills in the best locations, reserving them for those who arrived later.

I was in such an advance group with my dad and Uncle Al. Whether or not we set out on a Saturday or Sunday depended on the weather. Once that was established, we'd get up just after daybreak, load up the car with tablecloths, ice chests and sturdy cardboard boxes (prized items we searched for every Friday night at Bohack's Supermarket) fill them with coffee pots, paper goods, utensils and inflatable swim-tubes. Not long after paying the ten-cent parkway toll, we stopped at a local bakery to pick up a pre-breakfast treat of fresh rolls and jelly buns — delicacies my mouth watered for all week long. My dad, the driver, remained in his two-toned green and cream colored Chevy sedan while I chose the baked goods and Uncle Al paid. "Here you go BeBe," my father's younger brother would always say as he pinched my cheek and offered me the boxed treasures, allowing me the pick of the lot.

Al was my favorite uncle on my father's side of the family. Although Joe, one of my dad's older brothers, held a special place of honor with me because he always gave me a shiny new silver dollar whenever he visited, it was Uncle Al who sat me on his lap and laughed at everything I said. He called me BeBe as did the rest of the family way back then, but the way he said it was the most endearing. I loved the smell of lingering cigars and a faint tinge of blackberry brandy on his breath, the only liquor my dad would serve to his younger brother when he came to visit.

But what I loved best about Uncle Al was his knees. After we'd arrived at Casino Pool and hauled all of our gear onto the tables to reserve them for the legions of other relatives who were expected to arrive shortly thereafter, Uncle Al would take off his pants, neatly fold them across a beach chair, and stare back at me with his knees. During his army days he had an eye tattooed on each one of them.

A day at the pool wasn't complete unless Uncle Al winked his knees at me and the gaggle of other young cousins that surrounded him for just that purpose. He wasn't the only Cicio that caused a spectacle at Casino Pool. One day, when his brother Joe, of silver-dollar fame, came straight from the race track bragging about his pocketful of winnings. His brothers, Sal, Barney, Al and my dad decided to teach him a lesson in humility by tossing him, unaware and fully clothed, into the pool's shallow end. He was not amused. Everyone pitched in to help the chagrined patriarch of the family towel dry stacks of dripping twenty and fifty dollar bills. We kids never saw so much money in our lives. We hung around waiting for a wind to blow some of it off the table, which never happened, but we continued the vigil Uncle Joe finally put every last bill back into his damp pockets.

At some point in the day, someone from the clan was sure to put two fingers in his mouth and let out a distinct whistle that perked up the antennae of every family member. The "Cicio whistle" was a call for everyone into the pool, and a signal to all other swimmers to get the hell out. In rapid succession, my Uncles and male cousins jostled up the steps of the slide and made crashing descents into the chilly froth barking — arf, arf, arf — with mouths skimming the water like a pack of seals. Joining hands with the rest of us in the pool, we formed a giant circle, jumped up and down, splashed our feet into the center and broke apart in an expanding wave. It was like a circus act and our family was Casino Pool's star attraction, all other bathers parted for us as we walked triumphantly back to our tables.

Made of wood with long attached benches, these tables were located under a large metal awning which served as shelter from both the sun and rain. We usually commandeered the first row of eight tables closest to the open area of cement where young mothers could sit on folding chairs next to their playpens and baby carriages. Kids my age and the men sat on thick green mover's blankets laid out, beach-like on the cement. Since you couldn't buy these indestructible upholstery-thick covers — somehow acquired whenever someone moved — they were highly prized and passed along, from one generation to the next, like family heirlooms.

Elsewhere in the roughly two-acre pool complex was a bath house where closet-sized wooden stalls allowed us to change and shower the salt-water and chlorine from our bodies. Being able to wear a key for the locker around one's own wrist on an elastic band was a symbol of growing up. I longed to wear one on my ankle the way my cousins Al, Joey and Willie did, but that, my mother admonished, was not considered lady-like and besides, I was too young, always too young, as luck would have it, the second youngest of sixteen offspring, to do anything my teen cousins did.

I loved to watch them challenge each other, teaming up in pairs to play lively competitive games of handball, ping pong or shuffleboard. I was always under the watchful eyes of my mother or aunts whose job it was to keep an eye on the "little ones" while we were in the pool, on the swings or buying a popsicle. Leaving me stranded on the swings while my whole family packed up the car and was about to leave one day, was obviously the women's fault because the men were usually heavy into pinocle and poker as the sun began to wane.

One thing the women didn't have to worry about was preparing lunch since that was pre-made at home. Pepper and egg omelets, cold drumsticks, tuna salad, eggplant parmesan, bread and olives were brought from home and spread out on tables distinguishable only by their oilcloth coverings. My mom's was blue check, but Aunt Jean's yellow tablecloth was as welcome to me as Aunt Mary's red and green floral one. "Here BeBe, try some of this," I'm sure, had something to do with my evolving into a pre-teen chubette.

Though baby bottles had to be heated and coffee made atop sterno stoves at Casino Pool, when we went to Valley Stream State Park, the in-ground charcoal bar-b-que grills allowed for infinitely more elaborate meals. In setting out for that location, our advance trio stopped to pick up a couple of pounds of bacon and three dozen eggs in addition to the baked goods so we could start a fire and prepare breakfast for family members as they arrived.

Exiting the Southern State at the westernmost end of Long Island's south shore, we'd park and make many trips back and forth to lug the contents of nearly half our households from our cars to our favorite circle of tables. Laying claim to them with the familiar oilcloths, the three of us would go about our ritual tasks of opening folding chairs, spreading the moving blankets out on the grass and filling the grills with charcoal.

If it was a Saturday, lunch would likely consist of links of fat sausage with charred peppers and onions or steak marinated Sicilian-style in chopped garlic, fresh mint and lemon juice. On Sundays, the women cooked tomato sauce and meatballs at home and brought it to the park in cloth-covered aluminum pots. They'd set up huge cauldrons of water for boiling the pasta and stirred them with oar-like wooden spoons. The aromas emanating from our small little encampment wafted across the park, spurring onlookers to walk by out of curiosity, if not in search of a sampling. No hot dogs ever touched a grill in our neck of the woods, I didn't even know what a hamburger was until I went to high school.

After lunch and lazy naps for all the babies and grandparents, groups began to form for bocce, horseshoes and baseball. If we were too young to participate, we watched the adults act like kids. Many times, we were drawn into the mass hysteria our teenage cousins caused by playing unexpected pranks like water balloon fights and egg tossing, which they instigated when they weren't kissing their boy and girlfriends in the woods.

My cousin Joseph and I spent most of our time in the reedy woods, wading in the shivery cold rivulet Valley Stream was named after. We walked between the small rocks and plant growth on the streambed, looking down all the while following its winding path, until we realized we'd strayed too far from our family compound—causing problems for our teenage cousins who were supposed to be keeping an eye on us. Sometimes they'd find us dripping wet, because we fell or splashed each other, but mostly we got that way from hunting down slippery specimens like snails and tadpoles to corral in a plastic container and bring to show-and-tell the next day at school.

Sure as anything, our weekends abroad came to an end all too abruptly for us kids. Every Sunday night our wanderlust had to be put on hold until the following weekend, when, through three seasons of the year, our parents would wisk us away to faraway places—where Uncle Al would wink his knees at me and Aunt Mary'd give me a napkinful of homemade cream puffs—encircled always, by the familiar.

ACROSS THE STREET AND UP THE BLOCK

My family's house just happened to be right across the street from an elementary school; my mother-in-law wasn't so lucky. She insisted her whole family pack up and move within an eyeball's distance of a school in order to keep watch over little "Maichino" when he entered first grade.

Dressing for school one ordinary morning and not particularly happy about it, I was side-tracked by the grinding sound of a car's motor being pushed to its limits. From behind the venetian blinds of my third-story bedroom window, I watched as Mr. Sol Stevens inched his boatlike gray Oldsmobile into a tight parking spot in front of my house. Back and forth the wing-tipped sedan lurched and squealed — a good fifteen minutes — before its driver, my elementary school principal, was satisfied its low-suspensioned chassis was close enough to the curb.

Mr. Stevens and three other teachers got out of the car, inspected its sandwiched bumpers, shrugged their shoulders and headed across the street and up the block to Elementary School P.S. 75 where they worked and where I was a third grader.

This unfolding drama caused me to be late. My mother came into my room and found me still in my pajama bottoms. "Hurry up," she warned, "and don't forget to take your lunch so I won't have to leave work and bring it to you like I did last week." I stuck my tongue out behind her back. Scrambling out the front door with my lunch tucked safely under my arm, I came face-to-fender with Mr. Steven's Oldsmobile. The parking spaces in front and behind it were empty. Eureka — I was off on a mission.

With book-bag flapping against my knees, I took leaping giant steps up to the corner of Grove and Evergreen, waited for the crossing guard's nod, by-passed the throng of pupils lining up in front of their teachers in the school's musty basement and headed straight for the first floor. Slowing down to catch my breath, I opened and closed a glass-paned door stenciled PRINCIPAL in gold letters, and told the secretary behind a tall counter that I had a very important message for Mr. Stevens. She said he was busy and with a dismissive wave of the hand suggested I go back to my class. Hopping from foot to foot with the urgency of my mission, I told her it had to do with Mr. Steven's car. The old crone raised her eyes, sized me up with a long appraising look before turning on her heels. Quicker than you could say "park my car," Mr. Steven's bolted out from his inner sanctum.

Excited by the thrill of my self-importance, I announced he didn't have to worry all day about getting his car out of that tight parking spot since I had seen with my very own eyes, the spaces in front of and behind it empty on my way to school. Through a lengthening grin, the tall imposing Mr. Stevens praised me for my keen observation and patted me on the head before turning to tell the other office secretaries my important news. They seemed amused, but no more than I for conjuring up what I considered an ingenious ploy to get attention from the most important man, so far, in my young life.

Euphoric, I bounded down to the basement to join my third-grade classmates. It must have been winter then because the basement is where all the pupils and teachers gathered at the start of school days in cold weather, or on rainy or snowy days when the sub-floor setting became a chaotic repository of soggy wet galoshes and umbrellas. Gritty puddles filled with waylaid book-bags and lunch-boxes mixed with steam-heat and damp wool coats, turning the soupy underground into a sweet-dank sauna.

But the basement served as more than just a holding pen for masses of primary school children on rainy-wet and freezing-cold days.

Our daily recess periods were held there too, for many grades, all at the same time. Over the din of a scratchy Farmer in the Dell record being played for a circle of first graders, the whack-thump of a dodge ball smacking hard against cement and shouts of square dance calls through a megaphone for upper grade classes—the steady drone of unrelenting noise served as soothing background music to this kid's ears.

Those happy sounds echoing off the sweaty, concrete walls were stilled at the sound of four bells rung in rapid succession. It was a signal for us to drop what we were doing, line up against the basement walls and crouch down with hands over our heads. There was never any palpable fear associated with what we knew as air-raid drills because our teachers delicately protected us from knowing that we might be targets of enemy aircraft. These drills were conducted, more or less in a routine way, like reporting to the auditorium for polio shots—it was just something that was expected of us and we succumbed, like little troopers, without question. Of course, if we had a choice, we'd surely have skipped off the torturous lines waiting for polio vaccines, instead of having to watch others wince and howl through a river of frightened tears before our turns came. But we never complained and neither did our parents because all of this, we were told, and they were told, was being done for our own good.

The resounding ring of the lunch bell brought us back down to the basement where we ate lunch on wooden benches that ran along one entire wall of the cavernous space. The rough, open-slats of these well-worn benches pinched my bare legs as I sat balancing my bagged lunch and a 5-cent container of milk (chocolate was pricier at 7-cents) between my knees.

The school did have a cafeteria on its third floor, but it was reserved for some two-dozen students who qualified for free lunch. Wealthier kids like me — for my father had a job as a truck driver and my mother worked in a sweater factory — ate with our homemade lunches on our laps, a few steps from the noisy boiler room. While, by social standards, it was considered a superior position to be in, my lunches — drippy pepper and egg sandwiches or mashed meatballs left over from dinner the night before — forced me to juggle to keep them from falling onto the dirty basement floor.

Some kids, luckier than I, had high-class lunches like cream cheese and jelly or olive-loaf on seeded rye with thick yellow mustard. I always drooled for their lunches while gobbling mine down hastily because its messiness got in the way of my savoring its goodness. It's not that we had much time, after ten minutes, the next group of lunch kids would take our space on the bench and I'd skip off to join the games of tag or kickball that were already underway on the large expanse of blacktop floor.

Before returning to our classrooms, we lined up yet again in the basement for a stop at the boys and girls' bathrooms. Because of their location, flanking opposite sides of the boiler room, under street level in the bowels of the school's belly, these bathrooms were dingy and humid, sticky with airlessness. The doors on the stalls of the girls room swung free, without locks, very un-lady-like — so we always had to go to the bathroom in pairs, one of us held the door while the other relieved herself. I never did see what the boys bathroom looked like but we all used the rough, brown, craft-type public-school issue toilet paper and paper towels that were unforgiving against our soft faces and tushies and, in retaliation, we used it liberally to stuff up the toilet bowls and sinks. The stoppages and floods that resulted from our mischievousness served as a deterrent to use the bathroom as an excuse to get out of class.

In addition to the basement, the other indoor area where we congregated was the auditorium. When immunizations were not being imposed on us, it was actually a treat to be in the second-floor auditorium. On its raised stage bedecked with flags and speakers attached to a booming microphone, students regularly performed in skits and plays. I myself played the good grandma in Little Red Riding Hood and danced the Irish Jig on St. Patrick's Day. Every now and then, there would be a palpable buzz in the air when important guest speakers or kiddie performers came to entertain.

These performances were held once a week, on Wednesdays, when all students were required to wear red, white and blue for assemblies — the boys patriotically outfitted in navy pants, white shirts and red ties, the girls in navy pleated skirts, white peter-pan blouses and red scarves. Led by a color guard, we marched two by two, class by class, into the auditorium at the beginning of every assembly. When we reached our familiarly designated seats hundreds of little hands crossed hearts to "pledge allegiance" followed by the music teacher's pounding the piano to, and our singing of, "My Country Tis of Thee."

Assemblies were always held indoors, rain or shine, but recess was another story. Once the temperature rose above 70, we were allowed to line up and play outside in the fenced-in schoolyard. Back then, there was no such thing as gym, only play; no uniforms, only street clothes, no equipment, only Spaldeens. Most of our games involved those highly-prized pink bouncing balls that at least a dozen kids could be counted on to have stuffed in their pockets on any given day. We chose teams by shooting "odd" or "even" fingers into a circle of eager players.

On rare occasions school-wide events took place in the schoolyard too. Every spring, a May Day celebration was held to much fanfare. I loved to participate as groups of eight girls holding long flowing yellow and white ribbons weaved over and under each other until dozens of lofty maypoles were completely wrapped in ribbon. The boys, left out of this event, sat along the schoolyard fence and made it boisterously obvious they were trying to look under the girls' flare skirts as they spun around in circles. The girls were similarly left out when the boys played stickball or tug-of-war, and we sat along the fence and ooh'd and aah'd over their pubescent muscles.

At three o'clock when the dismissal bells rang, boys and girls together rushed home, wolfed-down a Devil Dog or package of Tasty Cup Cakes, changed into dungarees and returned to the schoolyard to continue our play. There were no formal coaches, and teachers weren't paid to oversee after school activities way back then, but even if there were, we wouldn't have needed them. With a great deal of insight and sensitivity for our young ages, everyone who showed up in the schoolyard after school was included in our democratically-devised punchball games, relay races and handball tournaments.

And at least once a week, when Mr. Sol Stevens left the building late, after a teacher's meeting, and walked across the schoolyard, he'd stop, look for me and wave. That was one thing I could count on ever since I was in third grade. My Principal knew who I was. I made sure of that.

PUPPY LOVE

Third grade was a turning point for both me and my mother-in-law: her formal education ended after that year and mine took off in a new direction.

I held the exalted position of being the very first of all my friends to get engaged. It happened in third grade when Leo Lucas presented me with a diamond-like ring he'd purchased for ten cents at Woolworth's under the Broadway El. Our teacher, Mrs. Tabulah thought it was so cute, she paraded us around the hall to show the other teachers her newly betrothed nine-year-old couple, but this celebration didn't last past the front door of P.S. 75.

When my mother relayed the news of my betrothal to my weary father upon his return from work, the atmosphere in our cramped five room walk-up, turned thick with silence. Lips pursed tight in annoyance, my father stretched his hand across the dinner table and demanded I hand over the ring. As I did, he vowed to run it over with the tires of his new two-toned Chevy Impala sedan. The thought of that big imposing car crushing the tiny (think about a nine-year-old's fingers) symbol of someone's love for me, was a crushing blow to my relationship with my daddy as well.

I was already in trouble with my mustached, heavyset father for telling Mrs. Tabulah that he wore a leather jacket and drove a motorcycle at high speeds around our block in the middle of the night — a time when no one would be up to witness it — a little creative thought I conjured up to impress my classmates while waiting one day for an "all-clear" signal on a stairwell landing during a fire drill. When Mrs. Tabulah relayed this colorful tale to my mother during open school night, she went straight to my father with the story. True to his character, he was not amused.

So it was with double disdain that he placed Leo Lucas' engagement ring into the scalloped emerald green and amber catchall box that held among other precious things, my baby teeth, some Canadian coins and subway tokens.

When I checked the next day, the ring was gone. I went outside to look beside the curb where my father's car was parked, expecting to find a flattened piece of shiny metal or pulverized glitter from the stone, but found nothing that vaguely suggested my father had followed through with his threat. And I wouldn't dare ask him where the ring was.

The problem I faced, was telling Leo Lucas what my father had done without scaring him away. I'd sensed the new boy in the class was sweet on me ever since he transferred from another school in the middle of the year. Mrs. Tabulah assigned him the seat directly in front of mine, and by the end of that first day, he turned around with a blushed smile and a black spit curl hanging over his forehead to offer me the use of his brand new box of 64 Crayola Crayons. Everyone saw. Betty and Patty Ann were envious, I could tell. We all had our own boxes of crayons some with 16 or 24 colors, but 64 colors all with unused pointed tips was like winning a Toni doll on the Ed Herlihy Show.

I have no idea why Leo singled me out. Most of the other girls were prettier and better dressed than I was. Maybe something about me reminded him of his mother who, I learned, had just died. He lived with his father and younger brothers two blocks from me, in an apartment over a store on Wilson Avenue.

Slipping inside the hallway at 930 Wilson, I rang the Lucas bell. A buzzer sounded letting me inside and I shouted "Leo" up the darkened stairs. It was a strange name, Leo — I only knew two others — Leo the Lion and Leo the Undertaker.

As my fiancé tumbled down from his second-floor apartment in stockinged feet, his two brothers followed close behind. They all seemed disheveled, with shirts hanging out of their pants and hair uncombed, I wondered if that was because they didn't have a mother to look after them. Trying to deliver the details of our broken engagement without making my father seem like a monster was not an easy task, but perhaps Leo had already gotten wind of the infamous story about the leather jacket and motorcycle, because he backed ever so slightly up the stairs.

I tried to stay as close as I could to Leo after that while we were in school. One way I managed to do that was by maneuvering my way into the small third-floor lunchroom where only a handful of students, including the Lucas boys, ate every day. I begged my mother to fill out the form that would allow me to eat the school lunch on the top floor instead of the school's basement, usually out of a bagged lunch soiled with grease. I always envied the kids that had normal lunches like cream cheese and jelly or bologna sandwiches on neat squares of Wonder Bread; mine were always drippy caponata or eggplant concoctions sticking out of scraps of Italian bread leftover from dinner the night before.

After much persistent hounding, I managed to get my mother to sign me up for the school lunch program (she was a pushover compared to my dad) even though it was supposed to be for the poor kids. Though I got to sit next to Leo for lunch, I didn't much like the smelly bean soups and dry cheese sandwiches that were served cafeteria-style on hard plastic trays. By the third day, I broke into tears when Mrs. Tabulah called for lunchroom kids to separate out from the rest of the line and I refused to go up to the third floor where by then I understood, I didn't belong. She paraded me down the hall, this time in a huff, probably because it interfered with her own lunch hour, down to the principal's office where my mother was called to bring me a bagged lunch from home.

Leo and I slowly drifted apart after that. I don't remember having another serious relationship until fifth grade when another motherless boy, Bernard Schiller, moved into the neighborhood. Of all the girls in our fifth grade class, Bernie asked only me to take my pick from the litter of adorable puppies that his landlord's German Sheperd had just given birth to.

Apparently, he hadn't yet heard about my father's motorcyle and leather jacket.

WHO'S SORRY NOW?

My mother-in-law was so holy she could have been the Blessed Mother's sister. She attended mass in Italian daily and went to confession all the time. Whatever sins she committed were surely microsopic compared to mine.

"Bless me father for I have sinned, I lied twice, disobeyed my mother once, took the name of the Lord thy God in vain three times, ate meat on Friday, had a fistfight with my cousin Joseph and knocked over a plant." What I didn't tell Father Ryder in the confessional long ago when I was a fifth grader was a sin of omission. I lied to his fellow priest, Father Zimmer, by telling him someone else was responsible for bumping into Sister Mary Kathleen's leafy potted plant and sent it crashing to the ground during a CYO talent show in which I was the star.

I could hardly let the lofty heads of my neighborhood parish think badly of me what with all the praise and attention I was getting for my Connie Francis-like rendition of "Who's Sorry Now." So when by accident, I careened into one of the nun's "prized possessions" which she'd stored safely away from us public school ruffians in the clothes closet of her Catholic School classroom, I told Father Zimmer who was managing the show, that the pot's shards of clay, moist soil and its entrails had been strewn across the closet floor before I'd arrived.

Expressing the right amount of indignance, I huffily followed Father's billowing black robes down the hall as he interrogated other performers in search of the culprit—all the while my heart racing with the burden of a growing lie. The thumping in my chest was not evident to others as I blasted "you had your way, now you must pay" into the audience, with a true appreciation of the torch singer's lamenting angst.

It was a relief that in the end, no one else was blamed for

what was clearly an innocent mishap, but I knew I would have to fess up to the gigantic lie the next time I went to confession. And I couldn't get away with that either because my friends would have noticed my absence when they came to pick me up on their ritual Saturday house-to house collection of our group en route to St. Barbara's Church for a communal soul-cleansing.

Since all of us received our First Holy Communion in second grade, going to confession on Saturday and taking the host on the tip of our tongues at mass every Sunday made us feel grown-up. What was particularly troublesome all during the week was figuring out how many sins we committed and what categories of evil they fell into. We'd been brainwashed from our earliest weekly pre-Vatican II Baltimore Catechism lessons that the seven capital sins were Sloth, Pride, Envy, Gluttony, Lust, Covetousness and Anger. Beyond that, we had to determine whether our offenses lie in the realm of more forgivable venial sins, or mortal sins, which were willful acts against the laws of God. "Thou must not bear false witness against thy neighbor," was a Commandment that could very well have sunk me.

That's why I couldn't confess my plant-deception to Father Zimmer for sure as anything he would recognize I was the culprit, declare what I did mortal for making a fool out of him, and sentence me to a severe penance. The tactical strategy to confess to Father Ryder turned out to be a wise move since he benignly doled out a penance of five "Our Fathers" and "Three Hail Marys." After that, my soul was cleansed of sins and pure enough to receive the Lord at mass the next day. And all my friends knew by the fact that I wasn't kneeling for a long time over penance, that I hadn't done anything really bad that week.

It always took me a long time to figure out what categories my sins fell into. The very first time I remember feeling guilty was in second grade when I accused one of the poor boys who lived in the infamously run-down tobacco road houses of stealing the nickel my mother gave me to slip into the Red Cross container that sat on the teacher's desk. I don't remember how I lost the nickel, it may have fallen out of my pocket into the street while walking to school, but I do recall wanting the little metal button that I could clip to my blouse like the other girls in my class in return for a donation. Could this be lust or envy? The dirty, smelly boy made him a likely target for my willful accusation but, he caught me off-guard when he actually admitted the theft to our teacher Mrs. Arness. I realized I'd done something really terrible when his poor haggard mother came up to the classroom to return the money and apologize to me. Though I took the nickel and put it in the Red Cross can, wearing the button had become, in my mind, a double sin.

Another time in third grade I railed against my mother for going off to work, leaving me without knowing where my library card was. Our teacher had scheduled a half-day trip to the Public Library and I forgot to bring my library card to school. When I went home at lunchtime to fetch it and couldn't find it anywhere, I blamed my mother, outloud. My Aunt Bea who heard the blasting shrieks of "I hate my mother" echoing against the walls of our third-floor flat, ran upstairs and scolded me for saying such hurtful things about her sister.

"Shame on you, if this is what happens to kids in public school, I'm glad I sent my Joseph to St. Barbara's," she said assuming her son was saintly, which made me even more livid. I don't know what I confessed to the priest the following Saturday, but I'm sure it had something to do with not "honoring thy mother."

"Coveting thy neighbors' goods" was another of my weaknesses, one I shared with my Catholic-school-reared cousin Joseph, thereby shooting Aunt Bea's theory of educational influence straight to hell. Like smaller versions of

Bonnie and Clyde we "filched" Devil Dogs from the grocery store and comic books from the local stationery store. Whenever dear old Mr. Di Miceli turned his back to us to slice salami or provolone, we'd grab a chocolate cake or cream-filled Devil Dog from the counter near the cash register and hide it somewhere on our person before leaving the store, turning the corner and taking a forbidden bite.

The old man lost a nickel at the most and since our families bought most of their day-to-day groceries there, we felt we were entitled to "extras" from time to time.

More caution had to be taken at the stationer's where the price of comic books ranged from a dime to a quarter. Our petty thievery consisted of choosing two comic books we wanted to buy, then slipping an extra one in-between. One of us would continue to browse while the other purchased the goods, so the proprietor's attention would be split among us. We were quite successful in amassing a large comic book collection and quickly learned how to trade them with other kids to keep our stash untraceable. I can't quite remember how I handled "stealing things" in the confessional, but am almost positive I found a way to dance around it.

Medical books and magazines like National Geographic gave us reason to admit to impure thoughts without much retribution, but impure acts were harder to wiggle out of. My first such experience took place when Alex Weiss tongue-kissed me during a game of spin-the-bottle. Feeling both titillated and violated — I scurried into the bathroom at Sylvia Perez' house and a gaggle of my good Catholic girlfriends followed in hot pursuit. Amidst the buzz of excitement and commiseration, we figured it's okay for Jewish boys to tongue-kiss because they never went to confession. Even Pete and Ray would be absolved more easily — as Protestants, they had general absolution. But how would an eleven-year-old Catholic girl who is supposed to remain chaste handle the perpetration of lustful acts imposed upon her? I merely confessed to kissing a boy and vowed not to be led into temptation. Whew! Close, but still not a mortal sin.

White lies were easy, and my mother who was a docile-type, was a push-over. "Ma, I'm going over to Linda's grandmother's house today" . . . when I actually took the M train to 14th Street and changed to the number 7 to visit the Museum of Natural History where I walked around the great blue whale so many times I could have made whipped cream. Or, taking the bagged-lunch my mom made for me, I'd make the sign of the cross before tossing it in the corner trash can and buy a baloney hero. She didn't know I got money to do that from my equally unknowing but always generous father who found a note waiting for him most mornings in the coffee pot (making coffee was his first chore of the day) with my request for a quarter. My mom had no clue too, I raided her closet and wore her clothes after she went to work, actually pinned up a hem in one case, then innocently returned it before she came home.

One of the few times she did catch me in a lie, it was a whopper. I told the girls in sixth grade that I had my period. I really didn't yet, nobody did.

I was queen Bea until my friend Linda's mother got a job in the same sweater factory where my mother worked. The jig was up when Mrs. Faucetta congratulated my mother on my "becoming a woman." My life was ruined. First my aunts recoiled from me for embarrassing my mother. Cluck-clucking and shaking their heads, they pitied her for having to put up with a daughter who misbehaved so much.

Worse still, my friends shunned me for engaging them in such a charade. Nearly a month passed before I felt comfortable enough to join them for Saturday confessions. They all watched to see which priest I would pick and how long a penance I drew. In a self-preserving act, all I admitted to the faceless Father Ryder was that I'd lied to my mother and to my friends, but despite a light sentence of two Our Fathers, two Hail Marys and a good Act of Contrition," I knelt a long time to show my friends . . . who's sorry now.

HOLIDAY SHORTS

Christmas and Easter were the only two holidays my mother-in-law celebrated with any degree of excited preparation, probably because they were deeply religious feast days in the Catholic Church. American holidays like the Fourth of July, Halloween, and even Thanksgiving were meaningless to her, but then, she never knew what it was like to grow up in a land of hot dogs and fireworks, costumes and parades.

A COLD, COAL HEART

My earliest Christmases were tinged with more nervous anticipation of finding a lump of coal in my stocking than the thrill of Santa's reindeer landing on the roof above my bedroom. That's because I constantly heard Aunt Bea tell my little cousin Joseph, that's what he'd get if he wasn't a good boy, and at that point in our young lives, anything that he wasn't, I wasn't.

As we got older the stakes turned more in his favor. It all came to a head the year a spanking new three-speed Schwinn bike was mysteriously deposited in our communal basement just after our family's baking of the traditional "cuccitate," two weeks before the big day. I was 11 then, Joseph 9, when I spied the emerald green two-wheeler with shredded plastic cascading from its handle bars hidden in an alcove near the oil burner. The gleaming trophy had a telltale bar across its length, a sign it was a boy's bike rather than the deep curve of a girls but I hoped beyond my most fanciful dreams the glorious two-wheeler was meant for me. My father, I reasoned, wasn't much into toys, so he could have made a mistake. Or maybe he won it in one of the many contests Charlie's Bar and Grill was always holding, I hoped.

If anything, the time had come for me to get a big gift. I

deserved it. Joseph already had a hand-me-down bike from his older cousin Andy, that, plus a soapbox scooter, erector set, baseball glove, a globe, Mr. Potato Head—everything a kid could want. I had weepy Tiny Tears and a permed Toni doll, which paled in comparison to the constructive and action playthings of my perennial cohort.

Because his toys were the ones we mostly wound up playing with, he always unfairly, I thought, had the first turn and last say.

So naturally, he was the last person I wanted to share my find with. I didn't even tell Roseann, my best friend and blood sister from down the block. Instead I lay in bed, night after night, mulling over the possibilities of the Schwinn's future, biding time until it was mine.

There was a double opportunity for that to happen since my birthday was five days before Christmas. The countdown gave me some leeway, if I didn't get it for one, I'd get it for the other I'd convinced myself.

When my birthday finally came and my parents gave me cardigan sweaters—rejects actually that my mother picked up cheaply at the factory where she worked—I was disappointed but the flame of hope burned on.

As the long-awaited Christmas morning materialized with the whole family gathered for breakfast and gift-opening in Grandma Beatrice's first floor kitchen, I noticed my dad and Uncle Joe quietly slipped out the door. My ears picked up the jostling from the basement stairwell. When they returned, and swung Gram's kitchen door open wide to present what was by this time the focus of my entire life—they presented it to my unknowing cousin who ecstatically jumped on the banana seat in his pajamas and peddled the gleaming steed-like charger around the kitchen table and back out into the hall.

For the next month, I begged the little stinker for a ride, but always had to barter away some priceless Spaldeen or skate key. Mostly I trailed him around the block on his rusty hand-me-down.

We remained tight, he was still my best buddy, but I never forgave my father for making me feel unworthy of such a special gift. His out-of-touch heart, I felt, was my lump of coal.

THE POPE'S NOSE

I don't know how the tradition started, but the favorite part of the turkey or chicken, for that matter in my family has always been the part that went over the fence last. I was five the Thanksgiving my father's mother, big, 300 lb, Nonna Rosa was invited to our house for dinner. Already drooling over what biting into the juciest part of the turkey would taste like when the part we called the "coolida" or rear-end or what's referred to in genteel circles as "the Pope's Nose," was cut away from the main carcass under my very eyes and ceremoniously deposited on Nonna Rosa's already full plate. The Buddah-like matriarch was beaming.

Not able to understand English, she had no clue why I bolted from the table and ran out into the hall, screaming in "high C" as I curled myself up in a tormented ball at the foot of the first floor landing.

"Mal de panza," a stomach-ache, my mother explained to the venerable old woman sitting at the head of the laden table. Hearing the falsehood, I wailed even louder.

My father rose from his chair and made his way out to the end of the long, dark hallway.

"She's an old woman," he said, clearly taking her side. "We'll get you another "coolida" tomorrow," he promised. I bleated louder still. I was a kid and wanted it now.

Left to cry myself out, I managed to recover enough to return to the table for dessert. My rosy-cheeked, well-sated Nonna, beckoned me over, "vieni qui," she said, pulling me close to her jiggly girth in a true bear hug. Taking my place at the table once again, I glared at my father with every forkful of pumpkin pie, feeling betrayed he'd chosen his mother over me.

My battle for the turkey's most succulent asset continued into adulthood. Even after we both were married, my sister and I made a coy game of fighting over the prized part every Thanksgiving. Whether the holiday was celebrated in my house or hers, our big birds would always be brought to the holiday table sans "coolida," prompting a kitchen-wide hunt for the confiscated treasure. Upon finding it, we'd make a big fuss of cutting it exactly in half, and swoon over each tantalizing bite. Our kids thought we were nuts.

Forty years after my first battle for "the Pope's Nose" with Nonna Rosa, I finally gave up the effort. The challenge became meaningless and my appetite lost the first Thanksgiving my sister was no longer there to share it with me.

PENNIES FROM HEAVEN

Whenever I saw a bunch of costumed street urchins walk up to my house and ring my bell on Halloween, I'd hide behind the nearest lamp-post. From a safe distance I'd watch as my father flung open my bedroom window, shouted "step back" and hurled a potful of hot pennies down on their innocent little heads. The big child himself took great glee in seeing the straggly band of trick-or-treaters pick up the red-hot copper coins, only to toss them sky-high, back up into the air.

He laughed like hell, thought it was funny. I thought it cruel, especially since I had to bear the brunt of embarrassment among my friends for his infantile behavior.

We kids weren't used to getting much in the brown paper Bohacks' bags that did double-duty as catchalls for Halloween treats. Unlike the goodie bags of today chock-full of a wide variety of tempting prepackaged sweets, what we could expect were a shiny penny or two, some individual tootsie rolls, caramel candies or squares of bubble gum. Usually children from one-child households were lucky enough to afford store-bought costumes, the rest of us used discards from whatever we could scrounge from our family's clothes closets — old shoes, pocketbooks, shawls, or sheets — the majority of us were ghosts and gypsies at one time or another. Sometimes using our toys, we could pretend we were Davey Crockett or a fireman or doctor.

At school, we'd dunk for apples bobbing in a big aluminum tub of water set up in the basement where drains caught the overflow, and if they were feeling magnanimous, members of the PTA would supply us with crunchy jelly or sticky caramel coated apples on wooden sticks.

We weren't allowed to wear costumes to school, but wore, instead, old clothes in anticipation of getting hit with socks full of powdered blue and pink chalk we'd crushed the night before, using our fathers' hammers.

Which is the only role fathers should play in their children's holiday.

BE MINE?

I was so happy my fiancè was absent the day our third-grade Valentines' Day art project was assigned. Leo always let me share his jumbo box of 64 crayons and I was excited to have sole custody of it, placing it squarely on my desk for all my jealous classmates to see.

Mrs. Tabulah gave everyone red construction paper, white doilies, a pot of thick white paste, a tongue-depressor to smear the paste on with and a small pair of scissors. Immediately, I knew what to do with them.

Folding my piece of red construction paper in half, I drew half a heart along its crease, then cut along the penciled line with the scissors. I opened the folded paper and affixed it with the sickly sweet smelling paste onto the backdrop of a large round white paper doily. With the remaining red paper I cut out an arrow, made a slit through the center of the heart and carefully — so it wouldn't tear — threaded the arrow through from back to front.

I don't remember the message I wrote to my beloved Valentine but I do know I made a lot of X's using as many colors as I possibly could to do so.

When we were done, each of us dropped our homemade Valentines into the class mailbox or took them home to family members. It didn't matter that I wouldn't be receiving a Valentine from Leo the following day because he wasn't in school to make me one. I put my heart into making his, and that, I knew even at such an early age, was an expression of true love.

What made it even sweeter was my father wasn't around to stop me.

RESOLUTION TIME

It wasn't always possible as a kid to make noise and get away with it. So it was a dream come true every New Year's Eve to be able to open the window or step out the front door and bang pot covers together and shake beans in an empty can.

Just before the stroke of midnight, our neighbors along Grove Street donned their scarves and gloves and hung the upper part of their bodies out beyond the window sills of their brownstones and shingled walk-ups to scan the heightened activity up and down the block. Back in the early 1950's it was unheard of to be anywhere but home when the clock struck twelve, probably because few of us could afford the steep cover-charges at a fancy nightclub.

Instead, we celebrated with relatives and friends, cooking

up big family meals and watched Guy Lombardo's countdown to the new year on our new Motorola and RCA TV sets. Before the official ball dropped in Times Square, we'd all celebrate in our own unique ways.

My family cooked "pasta con aglio e olio" and played poker with even us kids, though it was only for pennies, until the final hour approached. Me and Joseph would be allowed to hang out the windows with our moms nearby, waiting for the sound of the first audible merry-maker to start the cacophonous revelry that went on in spurts for the next half hour. Some people used toy drums or horns, and thick metal cowbells, others threw confetti out their windows, though they themselves had to clean it up from their front yards the next morning. My favorite noisemaker was a long wooden spoon beat against a pasta pot lid, which I found after much private practice, made the highest-pitched noise of anything else in our five room flat.

Some of the men and older teens would actually step outside into the frigid night air and greet each other with a great deal of handshaking and backslaps and, for the younger people at least, hugs and kisses. Every once and a while beeping car horns or sirens rang out.

Champagne toasts were only figments of Guy Lombardi's TV imagination. In our house, my father filled small whiskey jiggers with his favorite blackberry brandy—us kids' were allowed half of that—and young and old clinked glasses wishing each other "cent'anni," in a bevy of faithful resolutions that would be broken the very next day.

PART II - BUBBLES

Il proverbio: "televisione ha rovinato il mondo (television has ruined the world)

SLAPPING BUBBLES

My mother-in-law could wield a spade and thread a needle with undisputed authority, but the one thing I rarely saw in her hand was a pen. That was my instrument of power and I've used it, an early diary reminds me, since the time I was eleven years old.

Flipping through the faded green journal dug out from old boxes hidden behind clothes stored in a closet, I'm amused at the overly large, rather flamboyant cursive handwriting I used to have, and in awe of the resilience I showed against the crushing blows of what could very well have proved to be crippling peer and parental pressure.

Alternating flickers of recognition and disbelief jump from the pages leaving me to wonder just who this young writer was. My whole year in sixth grade was consumed with getting my period. I can't imagine how I ever got through it with my dignity intact.

February 6, 1957

We had a club meeting this afternoon and decided to call ourselves "the dominoes." Everyone has to be called by their nick-name from now on. Linda is Venus, Cathy is Angel, Phyllis Ann is Princess, Margie is Mousey and I'm Bubbles. I hate Bubbles, but they said it's perfect because I look like one. I want to be Dutchess. I hope they remember to call me that. I'm just not going to answer if they call me Bubbles.

February 12

Everyone went to the Chinese Restaurant across Broadway under the El and to the movies on dates tonite. Artie asked me to go but my mother said I'm too young to be dating boys. I see them all walk up the block from my window, the girls are wearing black dresses. I don't have a black dress anyway, but I'm not talking to my mother.

March 2

We played Hot Beans and Johnny on the Pony after school. Both teams wanted me for first picks because when I jump, the line goes down faster. Whoever calls me Bubbles, I'm not going to be on their team next time.

March 5

All the girls bought gold cullottes at Dean's Dept. Store for $4.99. My mother wouldn't let me have the money. I hate her. They all walked down Grove Street together with their gold culottes and white buck shoes on their way to the school dance. I wished I had a bowling ball to knock them down.

March 20

I told Linda I got my "friend" today. She told all the girls and they all wanted to come with me to the bathroom in school. I didn't play punch-ball because I told them I would get a heavy flow. I think the boys know too.

March 21

I told Miss Reid I had to go to the bathroom because I had my period. She asked me if I needed a napkin. The whole class was looking at us whispering, so I said yes. I chose Linda to go down to the bathroom with me and when we got down there I showed her the napkin and two gold safety pins wrapped up in a brown paper towel. She said she can't wait to get hers. I closed the door of the stall behind me and tried to figure out how to pin the pad to my panties.

March 23

Miss Reid gave me another napkin today. I picked Phyllis Ann to go with me on a pass this time. I didn't dance in the gym because I said I had cramps. Frankie, who's now Frenchy, and Artie, who's nicknamed Red, sat with me in the bleachers.

March 31

Oh, Lord, dear Lord! Why does everything happen to me? Linda's mother got a job in my mother's knitting mill on Knickerbocker Avenue and she said congratulations on my becoming a woman. My mother told her I didn't have my period yet and now everyone knows. They hate me. I know they hate me. I hate them too. I can't go to school or the candy store or anyplace. I'll never go out again!!

April 1

I went to school and no one talked to me. Maybe the boys don't know yet. I called up Linda after school and was crying, and she was saying I shouldn't have lied, and I was crying and said I'm sorry. I hate her.

April 5

I went up to Gates Avenue after school and the boys let me play Johnny on the Pony. Phyllis Ann still isn't talking to me. I hate her.

April 22

Theresa Marinello got up from her seat in the first row with a big red stain on her flare skirt. The whole class saw. Mrs. Reid whispered with her and gave her a wrapped-up paper towel. The boys looked around at each other and started to laugh. The girls were telling them to stop. I just sat there wishing it was me.

May 13

Cathy got her period today. She took Phyllis Ann to the bathroom with her and showed her the blood. I hate them.

December 4

Today I am a woman. I went to the bathroom and saw a long dark brown stain on my panties. I was scared because Mama was working so I called down the stairs for Aunt Minnie to come up right away. She said yes, this was it, I had become a lady, and slapped me across the face for good luck. I went downstairs and Grandma slapped me, she had a big grin. And when Aunt Bea found out, she slapped me too. My mother slapped me when she came home from work and pulled me into the bathroom to give me a new pink sanitary belt and showed me how to wind the ends of a Kotex pad around it. She showed me the secret place behind the airshaft where she and my sister hide the pads from my dad and brother. My sister tried to slap me when she came home from work but I ran away—she's too bossy. Daddy gave me a dollar, but he didn't say what it was for. I'm really glad he didn't slap me. I told my cousin Joseph who's in fourth grade. He rode away on his bike like he didn't care. After dinner, I ran over to Gates Avenue to tell all the girls, but it didn't matter because they already had theirs.

GATES AVENUE GANG

Had my mother-in-law known I once belonged to a gang she probably would never have let me marry her son. But ours was no ordinary gang.

We really weren't a group of toughs like the knife-carrying Puerto Rican Flaming Saints, or the slick white greasers infamous in our Bushwick neighborhood as the Halsey Bops or the menacing band of black Ellery Lords, but a rather tame bunch of non-threatening youths who were drawn to the corner of Gates and Evergreen Avenues after dinner every night of our young teen lives.

That's where Linda lived and ever since fifth grade, when the tall, blond, well-groomed eleven year old transferred into our class from another school in Williamsburg, a core group of us revolved around her like the planets around the sun. Hers was the universe we all wanted to be part of. The girls especially clung to Linda with the hope of somehow cloning themselves in her image.

She was a real-life Barbie Doll long before the perfect female toy was even invented. Linda's clothes were the envy of every girl who'd ever worn a hand-me-down. Her pleated skirts and man-tailored blouses were not only freshly store-bought and ironed with creases, but colorfully coordinated with sweaters, knee socks and huge butterfly hairbows synchronized to call attention to her star quality. For me, this goddess-envy culminated in Linda's freshly polished white buck shoes, which I'd only seen previously on the likes of my sister's heart-throb, Pat Boone.

I wanted those shoes as badly as I wanted my Cousin Joseph's bike. Cathy's mother had already bought her a pair of velvety new white lace-up bucks and since I was considered Linda's other best girlfriend, I needed desperately to keep my place among the satellite of girls that were fast honing in on my position.

Dragging my mother down to Broadway after she'd put in a full day of piece-work at the sweater factory was no easy task. She was clearly annoyed by the intense peer pressure guiding my feverous determination to own a pair of white buck shoes, and when she saw they would cost considerably more than she was used to spending on my shoes, a vast $5 difference between $6.99 and $11.99, she became just as determined in her refusal to buy them for me.

I was crushed. Was I for some reason less worthy of white bucks than Linda or Cathy? Did their mothers' love them more than mine loved me? Linda's mom worked as a garment worker just like my mom, and Cathy's was a counterperson at Nickel's Five and Dime, it couldn't be a matter of us not having as much money as they did. Trailing a few paces behind my stoop-shouldered mother, I cursed under my breath at how stingy and cheap she was.

I never mentioned my passion for white bucks to Cathy or Linda because I didn't want them to know how desperate I was to fit in, but in a snapshot of the three of us sitting together at assembly, with our identical weekly uniforms of navy skirts, white shirts and red knotted scarves, our feet belied the fact that I was different.

I'm sure the boys noticed too, because they always picked Linda and Cathy first in choosing up teams. I was always the third girl to be chosen for punch-ball and ring-a-levio, activities that involved hitting and running—highly prized attributes for bounding girls with athletic builds as Linda and Cathy had. When the boys did pick me first—to play Johnny-on-the-Pony, it was no great honor, since the onslaught of my thunderous heft was their motivation.

Our core group of Linda, Cathy, me, tall and handsome Stevie, Artie the tow-headed clown whom we called "Red", and Frankie the artist we called "Frenchy,"—nearly tripled in size when we graduated from P.S. 75 and went on to Halsey Junior High. I brought a girl into the group who lived up the block from me, Maureen—not realizing that she would add to the competition in attracting eligible boys. Linda and Cathy were smarter—they brought in guys.

Linda introduced us to four mostly older fellows who lived in and around her Gates Avenue apartment: Tony (Bongo), Jimmy (the Lawyer), Sal (Tutti) and Vinnie (Spade). Cathy brought in a clique of 15- and 16-year-old Sydam Street boys—Pete, Jocko, Ray and Ralph—who posed a macho threat to our comparatively immature and insecure elementary schoolmates. At the junior high school, we picked up Jack, Roberto, Sylvia, Ann, Michele, Alan, Buddy and Nick making our usual corner hang-out somewhat of a mob scene most every night.

Getting there was like playing a board game, each of us starting from different surrounding city blocks en route to the final square. I'd walk up Grove St., and collect Maureen and Mary Margaret along the way. We'd wait at Evergreen Ave. for Cathy, then head over to Linden St. where Buddy and Stanley waited and together we'd converge on yet another faction of our group. If no one was on the corner yet, we'd ring Linda's bell.

No matter how many of us there were, we were always welcomed in her house. I was in awe of the casual way Linda's parents comfortably tucked us into their daily lives allowing us the freedom to come and go as we pleased. — letting us use their closet-sized bathroom, pass easily through the two bedrooms in their cramped four room flat and open the refrigerator at will. My parents never encouraged that kind of open-door policy, so it amazed me that Linda's mom and dad accepted us fully.

I noticed that in Maureen and Cathy's house too. We dubbed Maureen's mom, "Mama Feeley" (her last name) because she sat around her kitchen table listening to all of our girly chatter and counseled us on how far our mini-skirts should go above our knees, and whether "french kissing" was considered a venial or mortal sin. Cathy's parents were always at work, so her house was good for blasting 45's at full volume and doing the stroll, slop, pony to the latest rock n' roll tunes.

Feeling the pressure to measure up, I begged my mother to hold a party for my friends in the basement of our house. It had to be discussed among the three judges — that's what my father called the decision-making trio of my mother and her two sisters who lived separate but among us on different floors. I made a good case for myself — the basement got little use except for Christmastime when we baked fig cookies and rice balls and hid big gifts, like my Cousin Joseph's bike. The only other times the basement was used was when my brother needed a quiet place to study for his college exams. This happened to be none of those times, so the three judges found it difficult to turn me down. Still, I had to get past Grandma because she owned the house, but I wasn't worried about that because I knew deep in my heart she adored me as much as she did the Blessed Mother perched on her night-table.

With her good graces and her three daughters watching over my shoulder, I spent every day after school for a week cleaning up the dust and soot that belched from the basement's ponderous black furnace. The brackish cement floor was pitched down to a drain just like the one in the backyard, and I swept toward it as I splayed buckets of hot water onto the ground. A faded gold couch emitted a musty smell of decay, and the mirror behind it was thickly clouded. I scrubbed like a charwoman, wiping down the tables, chairs cabinets, everything but my late-grandfather's hunting rifle which hung on the wall and was revered by family members as a sacred relic.

When the night of the party finally arrived, I felt for the first time, like the center of attention within my gang. A half hour into the revelry though, my mother shouted down the stairs for me to come up in the same angry tone she used when she found the curse-word in the bin. Hurtling up the steps two-at-a-time, I was met by three sets of angry eyes. The "judges" ordered me to clear the basement of my two dozen friends immediately. Suddenly, I heard no music, and I knew that some of my friends were listening to the embarrassing exchange from the first floor landing.

It was just my luck—Frenchy had gone up to use the bathroom on the third floor where I lived and absentmind-edly left a "mash" note he'd written to one of the girls on top of the clothes hamper. My mother found it, read it and shared it with her judicial consorts. No amount of crying or begging worked. I looked pleadingly at my grandmother who, I was disillusioned to learn, was too weak to stand up to the harsh determination of her three unyielding daughters.

One by one, Buddy, Big Mike, Jocko, Venus (Linda's ironic nickname, since it placed her clearly in orbit with the rest of us)—every single one of my friends walked up the basement steps and out the front door. They mulled around in the front of my house for awhile, somber-looking, as I, equally somber, stood by helplessly, my life clearly ruined.

When they finally dispersed, I walked out into the front gate. Patty, a classmate who lived across the street came over and commiserated with me. I was both touched and embarrassed by this kindness since it was obvious I hadn't invited her to my party. Hiccupping between sobs, I told Patty I didn't know how I'd ever be able to face my friends again.

The next morning, the bell rang and I looked out the window. It was Maureen and Mary Margaret. I slipped out of the house not knowing what to expect. Together we walked back up the block past their houses, to the corner where Cathy stood waiting. Turning onto Evergreen, we met Buddy and headed down to Gates Ave. where . . . Venus . . . Bongo . . . Tutti and the gang gathered. Just like always.

DANCING IN OUR SEATS

It wasn't proper, my mother-in-law once told me, for her to be seen having fun in Italy, while her husband was trying to make a living in the States. That's one reason she never learned how to dance. Another was her belief that only "puttane," or whores, shook and gyrated their bodies in such sinful ways.

My mother-in-law may have felt differently had she traveled to Fulton Street in downtown Brooklyn, as I did numerous times when I was a pre-teen. It was a trip I usually made with my mother on the DeKalb Avenue bus traveling from Bushwick through Bedford-Styvesant and Park Slope to the department stores—A&S and Mays—lined up near the old New York City Board of Education headquarters and Brooklyn court houses. At least twice a year, that trip turned into a pilgrimage for me and my friends as we boarded the same bus in a frenzy en route to the Brooklyn Paramount Theater to see our favorite Rock n' Roll stars perform songs we all knew by heart.

These forays turned into daylong marathons, first waiting for the bus, then waiting on line to buy tickets, waiting again behind velvet ropes on a ticket-holder's line, and once in the theater, waiting for the audience to settle down for the show. By the time the lights dimmed, and popular Rock n' Roll promoter Alan Freed stepped into the spotlight to announce the acts, we were so pent up with anticipation, we'd have squealed at the janitor pushing a broom across the stage.

It was the era of Dick Clark's American Bandstand, just after Elvis and before the Beatles when young female hearts dripped oceans of tears over Frankie Avalon's rendition of "Venus" sung especially to each and every one of them (I can personally attest to that). Among the two dozen or so acts shoo-bopping or yip-yipping into the microphone during the five hour production were: Fabian with his sexy spit curl, Bobby Rydell and his creamy wide-open smile and the sultry Sam Cooke oozing steam heat. We sang along with the diminutive, yet big-voiced Paul Anka to "oh, please stay with me Diana," and went "a Splishin' and a Spashin' with suave, finger-snapping Bobby Darin—never realizing that, cocooned in our local Brooklyn neighborhood theater, we were saluting icons of a generation whose songs would be played a half century later on CD's, oldie radio stations and rock n' roll revival shows across America.

The boys too, had their share of female stars to drool over. Lesley Gore, Connie Francis, Mary Wells, Shelly Fabres and Little Eva (with her charged-up "c'mon baby do the Locomotion,") beckoned for their love and they whistled and hooted their unabashed approval. But these solo acts were merely headliners, what really got us up out of our seats and dancing in the aisles were the Doo-Wop and Motown groups whose street-corner a capella harmonizing personified what could be achieved by poor kids with pure talent, an inspiration to untold numbers of young fans.

"Duke, duke, duke, duke of Earl, Earl, Earl," and "Yaketty-Yak, don't come back" were some favorites requiring a deep bass voice and reaching the high C's of Frankie Vallie's "Sherri, Sheri, baby," and Jay and the Americans' "Cara Mia Mine," was a feat all of us — boys and girls together, mimicked with every inflection.

The lyrics evoked universal feelings. We all knew what it was like to be dumped by a girl or boyfriend, so it was easy to lament along with Dion and the Belmonts' "Why Must I Be A Teenager in Love?" And most every girl came of age with Johnny Maestro and the Brooklyn Bridge singing "Sixteen Candles" on the jukebox at their sweet sixteen parties. But nothing got the blood pumping, feet stomping and bodies swaying like the Motown sounds that came from the girl and guy groups whose rivalry was evidenced by their dazzling coordinated outfits and synchronized dance routines. The Ronettes, Supremes, Martha and the Vandellas, Little Anthony and the Imperials, the Four Tops and The Temptations were enthusiastically called back time and again for encores. Breathless and visibly drenched in sweat, they tried so hard to please us ordinary kids with very little money in our pockets, and we were so receptive to the generous effort, we begged for more.

Some of the performers like Stevie Wonder, also had a sobering effect on us. I, for one, didn't understand how someone my own age and blind, rocking back and forth, playing his harmonica, could be so happy. It wasn't easy too, coming to terms with the death of the magnanimous Big Bopper who died in a plane crash that also took the lives of Buddy Holly and Richie Valens. The last time I'd seen the Big Bopper, he surprised the audience by strutting down the aisle from the back of the theater, sporting a big fedora, so full of life, singing "Chantilly Lace had a perty face and a pony tail, hanging down." For a long time, I was haunted by the reality of his being dead while his music was still so alive.

After the shows, it was a ritual for the Gates Avenue gang to walk across the street to Junior's where I stood salivating as I watched most of my friends bite into big juicy hamburgers with french fries. I could never afford a deluxe burger with all the trimmings—the only french fries I ever bought were wrapped in a paper cup purchased for a quarter at Greasy Louie's under the Broadway El. I always got through my friends' meal by relying heavily on the bucket of free pickles that was periodically replenished, and always seemed to be able to scrape up enough change to order Junior's famous cheesecake—which I could correctly say, I ate with relish!

Though it was a rarity, sometimes these Rock n' Roll shows came right into our own Bushwick neighborhood. That was the case one summer night when radio disc jockey Murray the K took his "Swinging Swaray" show to the Gates Theater, just three blocks from my house! It featured Jackie Wilson whose lamentous "Say You Will," was performed with heart-stopping pirouettes, high jumps and splits. We screamed so much most of us couldn't talk in school the next day.

My parents didn't know it, but when I was a seventh grader, I boarded a Port Authority bus with my pack of friends to appear on the Clay Cole Show in New Jersey. It was a weekend dance show that aired on Channel 13, something I knew my parents would never watch. I dressed up and told them I was going to a party. It was frustrating to see the TV camera's red light focusing on me and my partner Frankie C. — a moment of glory, dancing on TV — but no one in my family saw me! The following day, bursting with the secret, I foolishly shared it with my cousin Joseph, who laughed and said, "yeah, and I'm Superman!"

Today, as a senior already passed the big Seven-0, I sit beside my counterparts, now bald and bleached, with big bellies and double chins sing and clap and rock to the music of the fifties at Rock n' Roll revivals. When the arena dims and "Happy Birthday Sweet Sixteen" is sung, in silent unison, we all strike a match and bask in the natural high of the collective glow — celebrating ourselves and the generation we so happily shared.

And every once in awhile, I'm startled to hear one of my kids sing a golden oldie like — "Why Must I Be A Teenager in Love?" or "A La Bamba" and I wonder how they know those lyrics. They're mine.

FAIRY GODMOTHER

For old-time Italians like my mother-in-law, being a "comare" or godparent, was more prestigious than being a blood relative. Choosing one required much careful deliberation since it was a role that symbolized honor, trust and respect.

So my future mother-in-law would certainly have understood, the near riot in my house the day I announced I'd asked a neighbor who lived up the block to be my godmother for confirmation. My mother's mouth dropped three flights down to the first floor when I told her I'd already written Lillian DeSalvo's name on my sponsorship affidavit.

She didn't understand why I couldn't have picked one of my aunts or, if push came to unlikely shove, even my sister who, because she was already an adult, was a responsible Christian role model according to my mother's standards.

Hah!! She'd never seen her older daughter Rosemarie making out with her boyfriend Steve under the veiled shadows of the dark vestibule.

My mother hadn't a clue how determined I was to follow in the footsteps of someone who wore spiked-heeled shoes instead of house-slippers. Lillie, a red-headed, amply fed, Auntie-Mame-look-alike friend of my mother's struck my fancy and I was attracted to her like a thunderbolt to a tree.

In glaring contrast to the hum-drum gaggle of conservative women in my household, Lil DeSalvo wore flamboyant caftans and scarves, head-wraps and satchels like no other woman I knew. Everything about her was bodacious, from her half-dollar sized jeweled earrings down to her brightly polished toenails peeking out from red-feathered slippers. My dad, in his usual sarcastic way, called her "Diamond Lil," or sometimes, "glamour-puss" under his beer-belching breath.

He'd become buddies with Lil's husband Charlie, a meek wisp of a fellow, dapper and reed-thin, who could have played Stan Laurel to my portly father's Oliver Hardy. They socialized together with their wives, making a neat foursome for card games on Friday nights or on weeklong summer vacations to the Catskills. Usually, because I was too young to be left home alone, my parents dragged me along everywhere they went.

Trying to make the best of having to participate in boring adult activities like shuffleboard and bingo, I stumbled upon a unique advantage—the DeSalvos were childless—that's where I saw my "in."

Lil and Charlie lived in the last of four big apartment buildings on Grove St. near Evergreen Avenue, only a block from ritzy Bushwick Avenue, the wide-open two-way concourse for which the neighborhood was named and practically a world away from my end of the block where smaller two, three and six story houses were closer to the mom and pop stores along Central Avenue. It just happened my friend Mary Margaret lived in Lil's building too, and I used her as an excuse when my mom asked where I'd been, and also to explain to Lil how I just happened to be in the building and was just dropping by her highly coveted sixth floor corner apartment... Even before the majestic woman answered the bell, the seductive scent of Shalimar greeted me through an otherwise impenetrable steel door. Once opened, I felt as if I was stepping into the exotic worlds of Egypt or the Far East—engulfed by a kaleidoscope of piercing colors, ornate furniture, and atmospheric mix of scents and enticements.

The tight three rooms were adorned with gilded statuettes, crystal bowls overflowing with wrapped candy, gold lame pillows, and tactile objects' d'art that I was encouraged to touch and taste and explore. Even more enthralling was the inner-sanctum of the bathroom that I excused myself to go to at least two or three times each visit and examine under the cloak of un-watching eyes. In contrast to Mary Margaret's standard issue black and white checkerboard tiles, Lil's ordinary toilet was transformed into a Casbah of sweet-smelling rosewater and peach dusting powder with a plate-sized puff that I habitually slipped my hand into and patted all over the back of my neck and underarms. There were languorously draped tassels everywhere: across the frilly window and shower curtains and at the end of a long silky rope that hung from a shimmery robe.

A thick, plush rug hid most of the ugly floor tiles and matched the fluffy towels that I brushed against my face with longing as ours at home were so threadbare you could actually watch TV through them. If there was one tell-tale sign that I'd touched something in that room, it was the fragrance of Shalimar that followed me after I'd spritzed it from an atomizer also strung with a long, seductive, black tassel.

Most of the time, Lil and I sat catty-corner to each other at the kitchen table where a huge ashtray served as the centerpiece. With elbow on the table and hand resting on my cheek, I'd sit there until it got dark, listening to this empress-of-a-woman regale me with how exciting her life used to be until she married the poor sad-sack of a man, who for some reason, she'd held in contempt. Sometimes I'd be there when Charlie came home from work and felt the chill of a forced and empty greeting between husband and wife. It was a mock gesture I knew well, because I felt it in my own house much of the time.

She fed me too, between meals, which during my chubbette years I really could have done without, but the tempting sweets inside Lil's refrigerator—red and white parfaits, fresh pink lemonade and boxed chocolates, were as helplessly captivating as the rest of her house. She'd perk coffee for us—I was around eleven then—and unveil yet another goody from her stash of hidden treasures—a cupcake or apple turnover so rich, I'd eat it with my eyes. "Have some," she pushed, "go ahead, just another piece, I won't tell."

She didn't have to. Most nights when I returned from Lil's, I was too stuffed to eat the monotonous food my mother said was good for me. I was scolded but brushed it off. Maybe she was jealous the relationship I was building with her friend was becoming stronger than our own.

There was no way I couldn't have fallen under Lil's hypnotic spell. I loved the special attention she lavished upon me—it was so easily obtained—a response I had to work hard for at home. Lil was always thrilled to see me, whereas my family always seemed to question what I did, didn't do, or should have done. Perhaps Lil's loneliness, bereft without children and stuck with lackluster old Charlie, prompted her to confide in a mere 11 year old.

Her motives didn't matter to me because I was thinking of my own—that I could have the best of both worlds, the security of my own family and promise of the good life, if I made her my Godmother.

She was thrilled when I popped the question. "Does your mother know?" she asked sensing there might be trouble. I lied and said sure, figuring as was always the case, I'd catch the heat afterward. But Lil didn't disappoint. She was the best-looking, if not the most ostentatious sponsor to walk down the center aisle of St. Barbara's Church. One would have to have been blindfolded not to notice her manhole-cover-sized white picture hat and the wrap-around collar of her dress which could have served as a mini-race-track for Matchbook cars. I was proud as a peacock to see everyone's eyes on her when she stepped behind me and placed her hand on my right shoulder thereby making it known to all my fellow confirmands that she was my godmother. If my twinkling eyes could have spoken they would have said eat your hearts out.

Her gift to me was just as priceless, a gold watch inscribed to me with love. Aside from a gold cross from my parents I'd received for communion and a minuscule birthstone ring my sister gave me on one of my birthdays, I didn't own a piece of real important jewelry, the heavy kind, like Lil wore. But, I was disappointed it turned out to be a watch. What I really expected was a charm bracelet. Lil must have known I coveted hers, Lord knows I left enough hints— always asking for her to extend her arm so I could finger the heavy gold-weaved wrist band with dangling ornaments signifying every important event in her life. It was old gold and weighed a ton and in my own childish way, I expected to get one just like it.

Once she became my Godmother I didn't have to lie anymore about visiting her on a regular basis after school. She continued to make a fuss over me and I always walked away with one or another of her lively castoffs.

One day things got real personal when she saw me eyeing her pocketbook, a roomy, ponderous carpetbag—the biggest I'd ever seen a woman carry. "Here BeBe have a look," she said as she plopped it on my lap. Beyond its big clasp and yawning mouth were compartments filled with all kinds of surprises and my new Godmother watched with slit eyes as I inspected each one. Like a magician pulling one item after another from a bottomless hat, I began by opening a John Rogers facial compact and powdered my nose in its tiny mirror: there was a large-toothed comb and hair pins, though I don't know why Lil needed them since her short curly hair was much too sparse to hold hairpins and was in fact, meager compared to her largess—it dawned on me maybe that's why she wore so many turbans and hats.

A fat wallet was next, filled with photographs, assorted bills and lots of change, which I was tempted to count, but didn't. An eyeglass case revealed wing-framed rhinestone lenses attached to a long beaded chain and a makeup case held the brightest orange lipstick I'd ever seen. It too was John Rogers. Lil read my mind, "go ahead BeBe try it," I did and kept licking my tongue over its slippery surface. Next came a rectangular cigarette lighter she let me flick on and off. After that came the pack of Viceroys.

"Want a cigarette, Bebe?" she asked as she took the pack, smacked it against her hand and pulled out a long filtered cigarette. Lighting it up, she blew a provocative smoke ring in the air. I lit up just as she did and collapsed into a choking fit. I was only in fifth grade but I knew enough to go home and tell my mother. I was punished.

Some worlds are exciting, others are safe.

I rarely saw Lil after that.

BOYS IN MY HOOD

There was only one man in my mother-in-law's life and that was my father-in-law. He wooed her by strumming a mandolin outside her bedroom window and they married soon after. Clearly, this is one area in which I could say, I had more experience than she did.

When Ray Spivak came home for a furlough from the Navy to tell me he couldn't go out with me anymore because he got some girl pregnant near the base he was stationed at in California and had to marry her, it was my first experience with a love gone sour. As the white-capped, flare-legged sailor whispered this bit of unexpected news into my ear, I felt like sliding under the table in the Chinese restaurant where the Gates Avenue gang sat around a half-mooned banquet to fete Ray on his homecoming. What was doubly humiliating, was discovering all of my so-called "best friends" knew I was about to get dumped.

I should have seen it coming. Weeks before this calamitous news crushed my trusting heart, I'd been making excuses for Ray's not responding to my daily-sent, SWAK (Sealed-With-A-Kiss)-signed letters. Clucking in commiseration, Cathy, Linda, Maureen and Margie exchanged uncomfortable glances. Above all, on my regular visits to Sydam Street to visit Ray's mom and brothers who, I knew, adored me, I began to detect a polite chill, a probable foil to counter my cheery illusion that Ray and I were still steady as a rock.

What stunned me so—sex was something Ray and I never even talked about. We kissed and hugged and petted (he with me, me never with him, with clothes on, upper body only), so this striking thrust at manhood was something I didn't quite know how to react to without seeming immature. I was, after all, a high school sophomore and four years younger than the nineteen-year-old Ray. Why, I wondered, did he go out with me in the first place?

Before he joined the Navy and traveled beyond our Bushwick neighborhood, he was one of the twenty-odd guys and gals in the Gates Avenue Gang who dated each other on-and-off to find the right fit. I'd gone out with Sal, Nicky and Frankie C. before Ray and because our relationship endured for more than a year, it was considered solid. Going steady wasn't much more than being together when we went to each others' houses to dance, or a guy paying for a girl when we went to Greasy Louie's or the Chinese Restaurant like the one I was in when I learned the humiliating news for our break-up. Though Ray insisted on paying for me that one last time, I threw a few dollars into the center of the red tablecloth and walked out onto Broadway where the blinking neon lights of bars under the elevated train line intermittently reflected off my tear-stained face.

By the time I was a junior, I left Bushwick High School and Brooklyn forever to attend Grover Cleveland High School in Queens where we moved when my grandmother sold our house. Unfortunately, I had to leave behind former classmate Joe Camminetti who everyone knew I had a crush on: his brooding Sal-Mineo-like features made my knees weak. Before long, I befriended Albie, a blonde light-eyed German boy who lived in my new Ridgewood neighborhood. He taught me how to play tennis on the courts behind my new high school — an upscale game that no one had ever heard of in Bushwick. But when prom time rolled around in senior year I longed to go with Joe.

Since all the friends I grew up with in the Gates Avenue gang were graduating from Bushwick, Cleavland prom held no lure for me. Besides, I'd heard through the grapevine, there was no steady girl in Joe's life, and he still kept in touch from time to time, so I was sure he'd ask me.

Two days before the deadline to buy tickets approached, I was afraid I'd be shut out altogether when out of the blue, Linda told me her cousin George was looking for a date. Fearing total exclusion from this momentous event, I agreed to go with Linda's cousin. Problem was that I had never met him. From behind this tall dark George could have been George Maharis, the hunk from Route 66, but face-forward I could barely look at him with out wincing. I wasn't attracted to him at all, he, on the other hand was thrilled to be my date. It was a mismatch of momentous sorts, but I kept my part of the bargain and remained committed.

That stoicism turned to hysteria when, just four days before the prom Joe Camminetti called me to tell me he managed to scalp two tickets to Bushwick's prom and would I be his date? My heart sank when I mumbled that I was already going. It sunk even lower when he asked who I was going with. I was mortified, and angry. He asked another girl, and to make matters worse, she was a sweet girl whom I admired. There was no way on earth I was going to enjoy myself at Bushwick's prom so I bailed out on George twenty-four hours before he was supposed to pick me up. I told him that I was sick — and I spent my entire prom night curled in a ball, hugging the spaghetti-strapped eyelet gown my mother had bought for what turned out to be a non-occasion. That was major heart break number two

Number three happened when Lenny LoCurto's car skidded into a cemetery on Dead Man's Curve in Queens and he had to be rushed to the hospital by ambulance. Propelled from the passenger seat, I found myself splayed against the back wheel of the Ford Thunderbird that swerved on the road's icy shoulder, and called out for Lenny but only heard moans. Hurtled over the fence clear into the eerie cemetery, his broken body was draped across a headstone. Two months of operations and rehabilitation in a Long Island hospital had me running back and forth to visit my cast-covered, strung up boyfriend. His parents and mine had already met and liked each other in what seemed a prelude for a good marriage match.

We'd been dating each other exclusively for eight months after meeting at a Long Island dance club called the Mouse

Trap. On the night of the fateful accident, he'd just phoned his mom to tell her he'd be staying over my house because of a fierce snowstorm that was brewing. Our no-sex love affair abruptly ended when his hospital roommate tipped me off that he was jumping up and down under the sheets at night with his pretty nurse.

"You seem like a nice girl, I thought you oughtta know," the other patient said, patting my hand.

Being a nice girl almost caused Rick Maggio to go ballistic on me when I made him dump the packets of pot he'd brought back from Viet Nam. He was an old innocent flame from the Gates Avenue gang, but back from the war, he reappeared as an adult and we hooked up again through a chance meeting at Linda's house. He played alto sax and introduced me to the jazz clubs down in the city—the Village Gate and Village Vanguard to hear Dizzie Gillespie and Thelonius Monk—but the one thing my moral self wouldn't tolerate was the stash he secretly told me he was hiding in his house. Two weeks after Rick dutifully dumped the weed into someone's street-side garbage can, I told him our relationship wasn't meant to be.

"You made me toss a year's worth of pot," he screamed chasing after me as I high-tailed it down the street. "I did you a favor," I yelled back.

I was halfway through college before I was introduced to true manlihood. It was exposed to me by a dreamy Italian boy whom I fell for with a thud. We'd met at the Community Gardens dance hall in Queens and dated four or five times before he took me to a drive-in movie in his yellow MG. We were lying back on the bucket seats when he suddenly grabbed my hand and brought it down on his open fly.

Not having a clue as to what was expected of me, I jerked away. He was very quiet after that. We didn't talk about it. He took me home and I never heard from him again.

The closest I ever got to real sex was with Johnny De Vito

It was he who finally got to see me in the dress I'd bought for my high school prom, only it was four years later, at my college prom and all my gal pals swooned over the movie-star good looks of my highly-prized date. I was a woman then, a college graduate almost, when he parked his car in a dark spot under the Whitestone Bridge where he laid a blanket, and beckoned me onto it with outstretched arms.

Instinctively, I succumbed to his daring kisses and feverish fondling but when he dropped his pants, circling around in my head was the thought of my friend Lucille, who'd gotten pregnant out of wedlock and had to marry the loser who bedded her for better or worse.

As Johnny De Vito began to undress me, yet another admonition popped into my head. This time it was my mother's warning, the only one that ever stuck with me — "don't ever come home pregnant," and at once I pushed the heaving hulk away. My mother was dying of cancer and I was, at 20, still a virgin.

Much as I longed to feel alive as my mother's life was fading, something in me would just not allow this to happen.

Headlights from cars overhead reflected off the bridge's steel support beams while Johnny D. disappointedly folded his blanket and walked toward his car. I followed behind, subdued, unaware that in a few months time I would meet my one true love, from outside my neighborhood altogether and across that very bridge.

BEACH DAYS

The one time I took my mother-in-law to Orchard Beach with me and my children, she nearly drove me into the drink. "Watch them near the water," she constantly cautioned. It could have been my mother talking.

From our very first dip into nature's water-world at Lake Ronkonkoma Joseph and I were afraid of water sucking us in and taking us away. A half dozen old snapshots depict us playing at the water's edge, making sand castles and burying each other up to our necks, but none of them show us actually in the water. Even though our first exposure to a beach was at the shore of a relatively placid lake, we were terrified because our mothers' drummed into our heads it was dangerous to wade in any further than our knees. That warning plus signs my sister told us said, "beware of whirlpools and eddies" conjured up the horrors of the Loch Ness Monster in our young imaginative minds. On top of that, some kids who lived down the road from our rented cottage told us the macabre tale of an Indian maiden who succumbed to the lake's magnetic pull long ago and her ghost could still be heard screaming late at night.

 I fared better under my father's watch. He took me along when he and his younger brother, Al, went to Far Rockaway where I learned to frolic in the suds of the gritty ocean water without fear and ride the waves with my hands stretched out in front of me like Superman. The two brothers most likely were on vacation from their Teamster Union jobs when they went on these excursions because they took place during the week. Without their wives around, the atmosphere was considerably more relaxed than at the lake. The two brothers worked well together following the same trusty routine of parking the car in a lot about a block's distance behind the beach; then making a couple of trips back and forth to it to get a card table, collapsible webbed beach chairs and a heavy red metal ice-chest. They always opened the table in the same familiar spot under the cool shade of the boardwalk, spread an old oil-cloth over it, and stashed the cooler underneath in the damp, wet sand.

 Inside the chest was a chunk of dry-ice Uncle Al always managed to pick up from one of the butter and egg warehouses where he worked, and which I was told never to touch or my fingers would be pulled off. It kept the homemade sandwiches the two men prepared and wrapped in waxed paper before their wives woke up, as cold as a refrigerator. These sandwiches were always the same: thick rounds of salami and capicollo stuffed into big Kaiser rolls along with cheese — there was always cheese because my dad worked as a shipping clerk loading and unloading trucks at Lily Lake Cheese Company — the sole reason for my being able to identify Alpine, Swiss Lorraine, Meunster and Edam by the age of five.

Sometimes I got lucky and Aunt Bea let me tag along with her family to beach outings on Wednesdays, Uncle Joe's day off as a milkman. I don't recall what beach we went to but my stomach can once again hone in on what we ate — hard salami sandwiches on seeded rye with sharp gold mustard — I spent more time picking out the black, cracked peppercorns and caraway seeds than eating. Still, Aunt Bea wouldn't let us in the water for an hour afterwards because we had to "digest" our food first and though she imposed her "only up to the knees" rule, we managed some full-bodied dousings whenever she turned her back to tend to her baby daughter and my new female competitor in the family, Geraldine.

I can't believe what a flip-flop my mother did when I reached my early teens, allowing me to go alone, like an adult, to Rockaway with my friends. The poor woman must have tired of my pushing her to the limits of what she would tolerate from me. She didn't even look out the window as I fled from the house with a terrycloth beach-bag slung over my shoulder and headed toward Gates Avenue, where I, along with the rest of the gang, came out of different parts of the neighborhood and moved en-mass, like a swarm of buzzing bees, over to the Broadway El. We had to switch trains twice on the ride to Beach 116th Street, the last stop after Rockaway Playland. Upon arriving, we'd huddle on the boardwalk to survey the beach, choose a spot and lay down our blankets, securing their corners with satchels and shoes before bounding toward the Atlantic Ocean, the boys diving into the surf head first, us girls reeling backwards at the breaking waves.

Once we did get wet, and our bathing suits clung to our nubile curves, the boys included us in their horseplay of rough-housing, dunking and when the sexual tension heightened, underwater games of slippery tag. I mostly bobbed up and down on the opposite side of the breaking waves. Compared to the other girls in our crowd, I was the least like Bo Derek. "Thunder thighs," was what I once heard one of the popular boys say about my hammy legs. Trying to hide them took half the fun out of going to the beach, but not going wasn't even an option. I had to go, wanted to go, loved to go to the ocean. But while my friends paraded their size 8 shapes in the latest styles of itsy, bitsy polka dot bikinis, I was stuffed like a sausage spilling out at both ends into a spandex bathing suit that could have been worn by Esther Williams. When I wasn't in the water, I'd lie out on the blanket with knees up so my legs appeared slimmer.

Eventually I had to get up to buy lunch — the usual hot-dog, carton of greasy french fries and orange soda from Nedick's on the boardwalk, but I wasn't one of the prized group of girls the boys took after lunch under the rickety wooden planks to make out. And I couldn't partake in the sensuous rite of coyly asking one of the guys to slather suntan lotion on my back because, unlike the other girls who easily untied the strings of their bikini tops to expose the full-expanse of their serpentine backs, the elastic straps of my dowdy suit, criss-crossed — a virtual skull and crossbones warning — danger beyond this point.

Packing up at the end of the day tanned to a crisp, with grains of sand in my tote, wallet, and under my fingernails, carting a damp towel over my shoulders, having been smashed against the jetties, scraped by shards of shells, pummeled by the surf and filled with gallons of salt water, I looked forward to taking a long shower and slipping under crisp clean sheets of my parents' air-conditioned bedroom.

The Rockaways no longer had the same caché by the time I'd reached college. Then, I'd tag along every weekend with friends who had cars (I didn't, nor did I drive) and head out into the traffic jams that culminated at Long Island's Jones Beach. We had to be there before 11 o'clock to make it into parking field #1, which was closest to the most popular beach, and usually quickly filled up for that reason.

"Muscle beach" was what we called it, for all the hunks that played volleyball, threw frisbees and walked from section to section checking out the babes. Us (ahem) babes often set up promissory encounters with guys we'd met at a variety of local hangouts and frat parties we'd frequented on Friday and Saturday nights . . . "see you tomorrow at field #1?" was a mutual exit line.

If I was particularly attracted to someone I'd met the night before, I'd be worried sick he'd show up at the beach the next day, see me in all my thunderous glory, and be turned off. If I really had a crush on a guy, I didn't even get up for lunch, just stayed on the blanket with my knees up. Sometimes it worked, sometimes it didn't.

The one fellow who never seemed to notice my legs, despite a friend of his pointing out right in front of me that they were "too thick," took me to Rye Beach early on in our dating cycle. It was a test I passed with flying colors, though he didn't seem to know it was a test since he couldn't stop looking into my eyes. We undressed in separate locker rooms, frolicked in the aquamarine pool, went on the Ferris Wheel and into the Tunnel of Love. He paid for an artist to draw caricatures of us and we held them under our arms as we strolled on the beach, stopping every few feet to kiss.

We took our children to Orchard Beach, not far from the Bronx apartment we first moved into after we were married.

As if the ghost of Lake Ronkonkoma and my mother's haunting cautions suddenly resurfaced, I held each of their tiny little hands and warned them of the frightful undertow.

CHUBBETTE TO CHA-CHA

Like food, clothes were viewed as a mere necessity for Donna Maria, her wardrobe of dark and somber handmade dresses served to keep her warm and decent-looking. In that regard, we were like night and day.

It was Easter Sunday right after high mass and before my mom and her two sisters had fully assembled the big tray of lasagna that was about to go into the oven in Gram's kitchen when the bell rang. Just back from church themselves, my friends had come to call for me. Laying aside my hat, purse and white cotton, wrist-length gloves, I glanced pleadingly at my mother knowing there was time to spare since the day's meal hadn't even gone in the oven.

Preoccupied as she was, my mother nodded her assent but before I scooted out the door, there was a caveat, "don't get your dress dirty!" I flicked it off like a buzzing fly and ran out as fast as I could since Aunt Bea and Aunt Min were sure to stick their two-cents in. An hour later, I was all prickles and stings from the burrs that clung to my dress as I rose from the bottom of the dusty sliding-pond in the neighborhood playground.

"Are we going for the dress today, Ma?" I taunted the weary, hard-working woman every day as Easter approached the year I'd turned nine. "You promised," I reminded her over and over again. I was eager to make the 12 block journey south to Knickerbocker Avenue where the tony Betesh Girls' Apparel Store displayed racks of fancy holiday dresses, some stiff with crinolines and thick satin ribbons, others fluffy sheer like the chiffon styles that came in every shade of pastel with matching anklets.

The one I coveted and my mother agreed to spend a pricey $50 on, was a lilac creation that resembled the ballerinas' dresses on fine Dresden dolls I'd seen in store windows. I was proud to show it off to my friends, sashaying down the block, meshing in with them as we walked to the corner then crossed over to enter Grove Street Park.

At first, I only allowed myself to sit very daintily on the swings. Hardly generating any momentum with my slick patent-leather shoes, I watched as the boys ditched their jackets and hung upside down on the monkey bars. Just one ride down the slide was tempting. Giving in to it, the bow of my dress became wedged in a crevice as I careened downward, flinging me hands-first into the nettles below.

Looking down at me was my smirking cousin Joseph, whose mission it was to go find me. "Dinner's ready," he said . . . both of us knew I was in big trouble. He extended a hand and I took it. Using him as a shield, I limped home two paces behind. I'd hoped the fact that it was a holy day, would somehow subdue my bug-eyed mother as I hobbled into Gram's relative-filled kitchen. To some extent it did since she invoked "Jesus Christ," and "Mary Mother of God," in the same breath.

It was a long time before I had another party dress in my wardrobe, especially since my body was ballooning into an adolescent chubbette. My mother put her sister Minnie in charge of outfitting me then, because Aunt Min was a pattern-maker in the Seventh Avenue garment district and through her "fashionista" connections, knew where to locate age-appropriate clothes for young girls in half-sizes. She took me to a store I'd never heard of—Lane Bryant, in Manhattan—where she purchased with money from an envelope my mother gave her, a memorable bright orange chemise with a flapper-like dropped waist and kick pleats. I wore it to school the next day and drew what I thought were admiring glances from other fifth-graders in the classes I was distributing small wooden American flags to for the daily pledge. Only later did I learn I was being called a giant-sized popsicle behind my back.

Once I trimmed down and fit into regular preteen sizes, my mother and I took twice a year fashion forays to Kleins at Union Square or Mays in downtown Brooklyn to outfit me for the changing seasons in the fall and spring. She'd loosen her purse-strings and splurge buying me three or four outfits, shoes and sometimes even a coat. These shopping days were bonding moments for me and my mom, making the journey by bus or train through the hinterlands of Greenpoint and Williamsburg, or sometimes she'd even take me to the new Alexander's in Rego Park. Routinely, we'd stop for lunch at Chock Full O'Nuts where we'd both order a tuna sandwich and steaming cup of the "heavenly coffee a millionaire's money can't buy," my mother ever cognizant of the amount of coins in her purse she'd need to cover the cost.

Two prizes we picked off the bargain racks were a burgundy shirtdress made of polished-cotton, with a skirt so flair, it hit both sides of the wall when I walked through Gram's hallway; and a practically floor-length ice-blue leatherette coat lined in black fur with a collar to match. It came with a waist hugging belt. My youth and naiveté could excuse the garish choices I made, but mother who was considerably older and wiser must have been too tired to care, or just didn't know any better.

I still can't get over how I convinced her to buy me a fire-engine red, two-tier, chiffon dress with spaghetti straps and ostrich feather trim for my sweet sixteen. It was the first time I was actually allowed to choose something that was full-priced — markdowns were more in line with the size of her wallet. This time, she took me to a private dress shop on Myrtle Avenue, one so upscale she herself never shopped there. I cringe now, thinking how ostentatious it must have been, but my mom apparently saw the look of grown-up confidence on my face as I twirled on a pedestal before a floor-length mirror, stray feathers floating ever so gently to the floor.

I should have been going to the Stork Club with that dress, "but au contraire," my Sweet Sixteen was held in the back room of my father's watering-hole of the moment, Grande's Bar & Grill.

I was mortified at the stench of beer that my friends had to walk through to get to the back room, and at the way some of the older bar patrons guffawed at the stuffed toys being carried in as gifts.

But it was worth it to see the looks on the faces of my girlfriends, Maureen, Margie, Cathy and Linda—their mouths agape either at the spectacle I made or the chutzpa I showed. It didn't matter, I was Queen for a night and in the long run, I can remember every detail of that red-hot number, but hardly a stitch of the wedding gown I would one day wear.

OH, BUSHWICK, MY BUSHWICK

I tried once to explain what a cheerleader was to my mother-in-law. She was horrified at the thought that mothers would allow their daughters to wear short skirts with their "culi" (backsides) showing, and jump up and down in front of boys. It's a good thing she never had a girl.

Let's sing a song for Bushwick High
And a rousing good loud cheer.
With a song in our hearts
Let the whole world hear
Our praise for a school so dear.
In days to come, we'll oft recall,
Our fun, our friends so true.
So shout the praise of high school days,
Bushwick High we sing to you!!

I knew the words by heart but never got to sing them. My joyous, promising sophomore year at Bushwick High School came to an abrupt end when my Grandma sold our house, forcing me to transfer to Bushwick's long-time rival, Grover Cleveland, a near mile and a half away, in the hinterlands of Ridgewood, Queens.

I could have been moving to Australia, the move felt that foreign to me. Despite the lure of its majestic name, Queens was a place I just didn't belong. It was too neat and prissy, its spotlessly clean rows of two and three-story houses too much the same, its people more homogeneously German compared to the eclectic-mix of rumpots and scalawags in the neighborhood where I was raised. More than just being a Brooklyn girl, I was from Bushwick, a place that became as much a part of my identity as the way I walked and talked.

For the better part of nearly one-fifth of my life, I woke up in Bushwick, pranced and trudged through its square mile of gray streets, and fell asleep in its comforting safety net. It belonged to me and I belonged to it.

Others, more notable than me, were also spawned on the same little known streets of my youth. Jackie Gleason grew up on Kosciusko Street, and singer Julius La Rosa who was somehow related to the La Rosa Bakery where we bought our bread and pizza, were adored neighborhood legends, but not in the same big splashy way Flatbush was renowned for Barbra Streisand, Woody Allen and Mel Brooks.

My own personal brush with a famous celebrity was sort of once-removed. My junior high school English teacher, Mr. Marvin, was a less handsome version of his brother, actor Lee Marvin. I was in awe of that connection. Studying hard to master Homer's Odyssey I raised my hand a lot in class so I'd be recognized by Mr. Marvin and hopefully he'd mention how smart I was to his famous brother.

When I was younger my mother always half-whispered to me with a tone of reverence that Mayor LaGuardia lived along Bushwick Avenue, but I'd never been able to confirm that. I didn't know what the man dubbed "the Little Flower" looked like, or that he was even dead so I innocently and quite regularly was on the lookout for him as I skipped over the cracks and around the perimeters of that stately promenade. Surely if the Mayor lived anywhere in Bushwick it would have been on this main avenue with its pillared stone houses set back beyond deep-gated front yards, every other one marked with a swinging doctor's shingle, prominent signs the upper crust lived there.

Beside my own reluctant visits to Dr. Scuderi's Bushwick Avenue home/office, I spent many holidays sitting on the curb of that grand stretch of road to watch the colorful parades regularly held along its route. At eye level, I was caught up in the gaiety of crepe-paper festooned Red Flyers and baby carriages pushed by the Daughters' of the American Revolution, and less so with the tall, severe-looking banner-draped public officials marching to the beat of a John Philip Souza tune. My mom always brought a large paper bag along on these parade-watching expeditions. It was filled with Kool Aid and Social-Tea cookies and because I considered this such a treat, I hardly noticed most of the other kids had purchased their snacks—big three ring pretzels and boxes of cracker jacks—from street-side vendors.

It was a long, two-avenue block walk home from Grove and Bushwick to Grove between Evergreen and Central Avenues where, along with my house stood other mostly three and six-family dwellings, the local elementary school, a family-run grocery store, two large apartment buildings and a string of privately owned single-car garages. As with Grove Street, Evergreen, Palmetto and Linden Streets were all named after trees, while Madison, Van Buren and Jefferson bore the names of former presidents; DeKalb and Sydam Streets reflected the Dutch influence of Governor Peter

Stuyvesant, who, in 1661, was responsible for mapping out and christening "Bostwick" a "town of woods."

The hamlet's expanse was bordered by Williamsburg, with a largely Jewish population to the north, the predominantly black and hispanic neighborhoods of Bedford-Stuyvesant and East New York to the west and south; and Ridgewood, familiarly called "Germantown," to the east.

Although the Germans lived across the border in Queens, many of them found steady work at the breweries that skirted the northern tip of Bushwick near Flushing Avenue. Because of the pilsners' strong presence in our neighborhood, brand-name neon signs, tankards and posters of popular local beers — Piels, Schaefer, Schlitz and Rheingold — dotted the windows of its many taverns and mom-and-pop grocery stores. Even we kids collected the cardboard coasters our fathers brought home from their favorite bar & grills and the terms bock, malt and hops were as familiar to us as run, skip and jump.

We even knew the beer companies' jingles by heart, and with the same fervor as rooting for our beloved Brooklyn Dodgers, we sang-out their melodious ditties: "My beer is Rheingold the Dry Beer, ask for Rheingold whenever you buy beer. It's not bitter, not sweet, it's the extra dry treat, when you buy ask for dry Rheingold Beer."

It was advertising at its best, and as far as we kids were concerned, it worked. Instead of dreaming about becoming Miss America, all the little girls in our neighborhood longed to be Miss Rheingold. The monthly beauty contest sponsored by the Rheingold Brewery was after all, more realistically attainable. Local, pretty-looking girls like my cousin Anna could enter and actually be chosen by ballots filled out by me and my friends to become "Miss February" or "Miss July," and I could ride the trains into Manhattan and see my cousin's face beaming from each car and at every station along the way.

The train itself was a major lifeline for Bushwickites since many commuters including my father, traveled across the Williamsburg Bridge into Manhattan on the elevated J line we familiarly referred to as the Broadway El. Under the slanted light of its lofty ribbon-streaked tracks was the main shopping district where neighbors of all ages scurried to buy baked goods, shoes, pizza, went to the movies, ate Chinese food or shopped at Bohack's Supermarket. Other defining sites in Bushwick were its two vastly different parks: Knickerbocker Park was grassy and served as a nightime hangout for older teens. Closer to home, Grove Street Park's tar and cement surface was more suitable for toddlers scrambling up monkey bars. Overseeing the entire realm was the towering golden cupola of St. Barbara's Roman Catholic Church where Fathers Ryder and Zimmer christened, confirmed, married and performed the rite of extreme unction on just about everyone I knew.

And then there was of course, Bushwick High. I used to walk to it every morning with my boyfriend Ray, who picked me up on his way over from Troutman Street. But when he graduated in the middle of my sophomore year, and went off to join the Navy, got some girl pregnant and had to marry her, my focus changed from boys to books. I studied hard, so hard I alienated everyone in the Gates Avenue Gang because I was the only one among them to pass the Geometry Regents.

This newfound industriousness also caused my final undoing at Bushwick High. For extra credit, I took a job in the school's Attendance Office and within a few short weeks was capable of running its entire operation. Strategically, I took this position to give me leverage with regard to my impending move from Brooklyn to Queens since I fully expected to continue traveling to Bushwick High School by bus.

A troublemaker, I never found out who, though I suspect it may have been someone who failed the Geometry Regents, revealed my closely-held secret to the attendance secretary. The matronly sourpuss asked me in a superior tone if it was true I no longer lived in the school district, and I admitted it was. No amount of reasoning could convince her to bypass the school's transportation rules — "and that, my dear young girl, is that," she said with what I thought was a bit too much satisfaction. Deep in my heart I knew she seized the opportunity to banish me from Bushwick High School because I ran the Attendance Office more efficiently than she did.

I was angry. Angry at the attendance secretary, angry at my friends who turned me into a lonely pariah, angry at the snitch who complicated my life and most of all, angry at my family for uprooting me, ruining my social life and dashing my dream to sing a song to Bushwick High.

Grandma and Aunt Minnie moved into an apartment on the perimeter of the old neighborhood. Aunt Bea and Uncle Joe bought a house in Jamaica, Queens and eventually we moved to nearby Ridgewood. Oh, I did take the bus back to the old neighborhood, but it just wasn't the same. I felt strangely, like an outsider. Without Ray or specific reasons to stay in touch, like going to birthday parties, my life began to turn in a different direction and I made the trip back less and less often.

There was a last chance for me to return to Bushwick High when I was asked to go to the senior prom, but that too, turned into another lost opportunity that never materialized.

Five decades have passed since I left the old neighborhood and I've never been back. I may have left Bushwick, but it never left me.

COLLAPSE OF THE HOUSE OF CARDS

I can just imagine how difficult it must have been for my mother-in-law to travel 4,000 miles to start a new life in a strange land. For me, moving twenty blocks was just as traumatic.

My life was humming along nicely, I'd just started my sophomore year at Bushwick High School and was adjusting as a budding-adult on the expanding social scene when my parents delivered the crushing news that ended the world as I knew it. Grandma had sold the house — her house — our house — the only one I'd ever lived in — and we had to move.

Blockbusters, my mother told me, were the reason. They were a new species of real-estate lowlifes who apparently made their living by frightening innocent, elderly homeowners like my widowed Grandmother, into selling their houses because the impending encroachment of minority populations and their accompanying slums from Bedford-Styvesant into Bushwick would send property values plummeting.

"This house is the only savings your Grandma has," my mother said.

I listened carefully, but quickly reverted to teenage behavior. Thundering down two flights of stairs screaming like a crazed animal, banging both sides of the walls with my fists, I reached Gram's apartment, flung open the door and threw myself at her mercy.

"You can't do this to me," I sobbed in what I'm sure Aunt Bea would have considered my best rendition of Sarah Bernhardt yet. The diminutive mild-mannered matriarch was sympathetic, patted the tear-soaked head lying on her lap, but was powerless, she explained, to rescind the contract that had already been signed on the dotted line by her very own gnarled and shriveled hand.

I should have known our house of cards would fall. Aunt Bea and Uncle Joe started the wrecking ball swinging six months before by buying their own single-family house all the way out in the wilds of Jamaica, Queens. I even burned my hand helping them steam the yellowed paper off the walls in their new six-room dormered Cape Cod, how could I have been so oblivious to think there would be no further scalding repercussions for me as a result of their moving away?

A family called Viola quickly rented Aunt Bea's former middle-floor apartment, causing those of us who remained, to feel cut off from each other for the very first time. Living with strangers was awkward, I for one had to change my unselfconscious habits of tumbling down the stairs in my pajamas, throwing temper tantrums and bursting into echo-producing songs. In a matter of months the security of growing up with extended family members enmeshed in near every facet of my daily life, was eroding and all I could do was pine for the way it used to be.

Before long, we began to think of ourselves not as a whole unit, but individual pieces of the pie, as we turned to assess our own separate living quarters behind closed doors. Mine was a five room railroad flat with a kitchen the size of today's modern bathrooms. All five of us couldn't squeeze into it without touching each other.

A grey formica kitchen table pushed up against the back of the dining room wall was where we took turns sitting down to eat breakfast. My dad was off to his job at the cheese warehouse downtown on Houston Street by six; my sister left for midtown where she worked as a secretary at J.C. Penny's around eight. I went to school at 8:30 and my brother headed off to study at St. John's University School of Pharmacy after that. My mother usually ate upright, leaning her back against the sink, before heading out to the local knitting mill where she sewed ribbon bindings on sweaters.

On the other side of the kitchen's entrance was a tall broom closet. In the days before everyone owned a vacuum cleaner, it held a dust mop and long-handled carpet cleaner, the ironing board and a few of my brother's baseball bats. Next to it stood a Bendix washing machine with an old-fashioned ringer. My mother ran each soaking piece of wet laundry through that unwieldy contraption before stretching them out on one of two clotheslines, which hung like sagging tightropes from our kitchen and dining room windows to a telephone pole in the backyard.

Wedged tightly between the Bendix and far wall was a Frigidaire refrigerator already dwarfed by my height with heavy metal shelves and a shoe box-sized freezer, so caked with ice, it looked like an igloo. The fridge's door had a handle much like a car door's, and opening it wide just cleared the adjacent sink and washtub which, covered by a white enamel drainboard, always held Flintstone jelly glasses along with my father's empty beer bottles. Occasionally, hot water came out of the sink's ice-cold spigots.

Between the sink and window, a Hotpoint stove turned out what had to be the best meals this side of Grove Street. I don't know how my mother managed to cook big roasts and trays of lasagne in such a tiny space, since opening the oven door took up a good portion of the kitchen.

Facing the stove a cupboard rose from floor to ceiling. Behind its wood framed doors, chipped in spots from layers upon layers of thick-coated paint, were dishes, pots, food, utensils, scouring pads and sometimes even a stray mouse. Fortunately, my father's work in a cheese warehouse made him an expert at trapping them.

Dinner, every night was served in the next room, around the fine mahogany dining table covered with a plastic cloth. We could have still been eating separately in the kitchen for all the conversation that took place. What kept our joint attention was watching the slapstick antics of the Three Stooges on our the new 12" black and white television set. What we did share, the five of us, as a family every night, was laughter every time Moe bopped Curley on the head.

It's no wonder I didn't find out about Gram selling the house, there was such little communication among us.

After dinner was when everyone talked — downstairs on the first floor in Gram's kitchen where we gathered for coffee, or when weather permitted, outside in the front gate. Most likely I was out with my friends when they discussed selling the house. Would it have made a difference if I was there? Maybe I could have talked Gram out of it — she always thought I was smart. I wonder who encouraged her to sell? Was it Aunt Min? My Mom or Dad? Or was Aunt Bea still involved in our household business from far away.

My parents would never buy a house, I knew that. My dad was too much of a saver to make an investment like that, and he wasn't the handyman type. He was the drinking type, so we'd have to factor in proximity to a neighborhood saloon wherever we landed.

Sure as I predicted, the five-room, ground floor apartment my parents signed a two-year lease for was conveniently located around the corner from a German Hofbrau. It lay clear across the Brooklyn border in Ridgewood, Queens, but so far away from my cousin in Jamaica, Queens, we had to travel over an hour, by bus and train, to visit him. As far as I was concerned we may as well have moved to another country.

With my married sister and brother happily ensconced in their own Queens apartments, she in Glendale, he in Cypress Hills, and without Gram and Aunt Min to drop in on every day, our familial vortex had pitifully whittled down to mom, dad and me. It was no consolation that I was finally able to have my own room with my very own door because there was no longer anyone around to invade my privacy.

Worst yet was leaving the Gates Avenue Gang, just when it was so important to be together, during high school when there were basketball games, proms and confraternity dances to go to. The Gates Avenue hangout was only two bus rides away (with a transfer), but it seemed I was always the one shuttling back and forth because that's where the action was. My friends had no reason to visit me in my spanking clean but ho-hum tree-lined neighborhood. I would have loved to see that happen though, all twenty of them descending on me at once would have had my starchy neighbors running for smelling salts!

So many things changed all at once. I had to apply for a Queens library card and relearn, like a baby taking its first steps, where to stake out a fresh supply of Irving Wallace novels. I joined a new Roman Catholic parish, the Lady of the Miraculous Medal, and attended mass — gasp — by myself for the very first time in my life! Oh, how I missed the comfort of St. Barbara's recognizable saints and faces. It took a long time for me to make friends at my new high school, Grover Cleveland, it was Bushwick's rival, and because of that put me in a deeper dilemma as to where my loyalty lay.

To my utter surprise, ever so slowly, I began to adapt. Eventually I was forced to cut my ties to places and people I'd lived with through the age of fifteen, and threw myself into my studies to the point of being called a "brown-nose."

It didn't seem so at the time, but moving away from the familiar helped me find my own identity and for the first time ever, I began to trust my own judgment.

Years later when it dawned on me to ask, I learned through the sub-rosa murmurs of the family grapevine that Gram made a nice profit on the sale of 140 Grove St. What her husband originally paid $6000 for in 1939 she sold in 1961 for $14,000. It may not have made her popular with the neighbors, but soon after we left, they did too.

PART III—BEATRICE

Il proverbio: Una mamma può crescere dieci figli ma dieci figli non possono occuparsi di una mamma (one mother can raise ten children but ten children can't take care of one mother)

THE THREE JUDGES

Unlike my meek mother, had "Mamma Maria" lived at our house in the 1950's, I'm sure she would have stood up to my father and made him beg for mercy.

Daddy was not usually in a good mood when he referred to mamma and her two sisters as the "three judges." He typically used this term to shield himself against the triple onslaught of rebuke the three blood-relatives leveled against him whenever there was reason to take sides.

In our household that meant practically all the time. My Archie Bunker-like father, was not one to listen to reason. Being a cantankerous sort, his way was always the right way, and often expressed it in a loud enough voice in our top-floor apartment for my aunts, downstairs, to hear.

"Here they go again, the three judges, telling me what to do," my father would rail in a last ditch effort to save face in a battle he knew he'd already lost. Lucky for my mom her two younger sisters, who continually squabbled amongst themselves, put their own differences aside to present a united front against their boisterous brother-in-law. "Mind your own business," he'd shoot back at them, pointing his finger in their stoic faces.

For their part, they likely held back a lot not to make trouble for their sister.

Alone my mother was a timid, powerless woman, good-natured, without enemies, easily brought to tears. Her gentle nature was very much like that of her own mother, my Grandma Beatrice. But Aunt Bea and Aunt Minnie's personalities were made of stronger stuff. The two of them had more than enough bravura to make up for their older sister's inherent weaknesses, and much to my father's consternation, they used it whether they were asked to or not.

Being the oldest and of course, married to my Dad, my Mom was deemed Judge #1.

Judge #2, Aunt Minnie, was referred to by people outside our family as the spinster (family members themselves wouldn't dare risk calling her that). Closest in age to my mom by five years, Aunt Min lived with Grandma in a spacious three room, ground floor apartment where the rest of us dropped in at will to visit Grandma throughout the day. This lack of privacy could conceivably be the reason why Aunt Minnie was so easily annoyed.

I'm sure my continual presence in Grandma's kitchen contributed to that, especially on Saturday nights when I'd sit on the skirted rocking chair and watch Aunt Min give herself a bath at the kitchen sink. With scrupulous intensity she'd lather up a small washrag and make small hard circles of thick white foam on her face, then her neck, armpits and feet.

Following her into the bedroom, I'd jump on one of the twin beds she shared with Gram, watching intently her search in the wood cupboard for a fresh pair of stockings, silk undies and, compared to my mother, a rather small-sized bra.

"Are my seams straight?" she'd ask, at last justifying my presence during her weekly transformation from lowly pattern-maker to elegant lady and hopeful lure for the minions of prospective dance partners awaiting her arrival at the Roseland Ballroom in Manhattan. She was the glamorous sister, "glamor-puss" my dad called her behind her back.

Mom, Gram and Aunt Bea wore house-dresses most of the time, so watching Aunt Min step high-heeled into a crinolined dress, as flare-around as those worn in the Harvest Moon Ball, presented a role-model that held the promise of magic.

Next was her crystal costume and gold jewelry, all chunky and sparkly. She allowed me to finger each ring, necklace, earring and bracelet, while laying them on the bureau for her inspection and selection. There were no rubies or diamonds among Aunt Min's baubles but to me, her sizeable gems were the most precious items in our entire house.

Then out came her make-up case. Normally, it would take Aunt Min a half-hour more, again by the cracked mirror over the kitchen sink to apply pancake powder, draw arches over her non-existent eyebrows, and tissue-blot her thickly colored lips. Just before a flurry of lady friends came to pick her up she'd wrap herself up in a glossy black lamb's wool coat and spin around for the mirror's and my approval. A final act in this ablution was a baptismal rite with Chanel No. 5. Twinkling at me, she'd walk into the frosty night, her scent lingering in my dreams.

Judge #3, Aunt Bea, my namesake and godmother, rarely bubbled with such joy. Her long-suffering gloom may have stemmed from being too smart for her own good. The youngest of the three sisters, she held the most promise of going onto college and having a career—something her illiterate, strict Sicilian-born father didn't see the need for—so Aunt Bea's formal education ended, just as her older sisters did, after eighth grade.

Swallowing her intellectual-prowess with a certain degree of bitterness, Aunt Bea doted instead on her marriage to Uncle Joe, a handsome soldier who fought on the Pacific front during WW II; her two children, Joseph (my cohort and nemesis) and Geraldine, and her spit-shined four room apartment. Of the three families who lived in Grandma's three-story dwelling, Aunt Bea's pots shined the brightest, her curtains were the crispest and hallway was the neatest. She was the only one in the house to buy "real" art for her living room, it was a reproduction of Gainesborough's "Blue Boy" but none of us knew that—all we knew was that it was a painting—and in our house that's all it took to make it special.

Aunt Bea did something else that I observed closely—she helped my Cousin Joseph with his homework. It was quite the opposite in my household where I'd usually teach my mother what I'd learned in school. I was jealous of this special relationship Aunt Bea had with her kids. Try as she may to separate her neatly-bound family of four from the rest of the extended family, I always seemed to worm my way in.

Sarah Bernhardt she called me, because my sobbing tears and banging feet were always so dramatic. Hey, I was just a little kid, what did she expect? "Oh, you think you know everything," she'd say when I'd defend myself in some sort of scrap with her precious son. We locked horns a lot because of my "influence" on Joseph and it always amazed me that Aunt Bea challenged me as if I were her equal.

The strongest test of our tenacious wills usually occurred on Wednesdays, the day Uncle Joe had off from his job as a milkman. From the beginning of the week, I'd keep my antennae up to hear what the happy foursome's plans would be for their midweek outing, to the beach, the zoo, a picnic, or crabbing. Everyone in my family worked, so by default Grandma and Aunt Bea always looked after me.

On Wednesdays, as soon as the front gate swung open, I'd station myself behind the venetian blinds of my third-floor bedroom window, and longingly watch Uncle Joe and Joseph load their Pontiac sedan with beach chairs and coolers, blankets and floats. They avoided looking up at me, though I knew at least Joseph was aware of my weekly vigil. It wasn't until Aunt Bea came out, that my fate would be decided. If she looked up and waved me on down, I'd grab my already packed beach-bag and slide down the banister. If she slipped into the car's front seat without a glance up, I knew I'd have to spend the rest of the long hot summer day playing cards with Gram at her kitchen table.

If Aunt Min introduced me to elegance and glamour, Aunt Bea's life-long lessons were knowledge and power.

Judge #1 wasn't like either of the other two. My mother's passive personality was probably the reason my father tried to dominate her, but Aunt Bea and Aunt Min's "putting their two cents in", rankled my very macho dad to no end.

It all came to a head one night when I was sent downstairs to my Cousin Joseph's house and was told not to move from there. My father had gotten off from work early that day and he thought he'd surprise my mother by taking her out to lunch. But when he got to the sweater factory where she worked and saw her walk out the door with her male boss, he held back to spy on her, lurking behind signposts and between doorways.

"You lit a cigarette and smoked!" he charged that night at the dinner table.

"I always smoke on my lunch break," she replied, defending herself.

"Well you never smoke when you walk with me! Besides, you were laughing," he said, jumping up from the table throwing his chair out from under him. That's when my brother Willie and sister Rosemarie told me to go downstairs. On my way down, Aunt Bea and Aunt Min ran past me on their way up. I looked back to see the door snap firmly behind them.

Raucous accusations hurtled back and forth while Joseph and I lay on our stomachs coloring a floor below. He was six,

I was eight, we didn't talk about what was going on overhead, but silently chose different crayons from the same pack when the sound of furniture crashing and rumbling footsteps brought us to our scared little feet.

Rosemarie came down to stay with us and we stood behind her as she listened, shakily, through the slightly open door. Her eyes were red and she kept looking up the stairs. Stroking the back of my head, she said not to worry, "go color," but that was no longer possible.

A week later I was at the supermarket with my mother when my ears perked up. I heard her bantering with the man who was weighing the fruit and took note that she smiled at him. Walking home together, I asked why she was talking to that man.

She stopped, closed her eyes and moaned.

That night I lay in bed wondering if I should tell my father.

WAITING IN THE WINGS

Girly things like dressing up and using make-up, having crushes on boys and swooning over movie stars were dismissed as foolish by my mother-in-law. Not having had a sister may have been the reason why.

She never took center stage, my sister; her role was very much hidden in the wings while scenes of our mercurial family life erupted around her. Even when, as a teenager, she was hit by a taxicab on Knickerbocker Avenue, she ran all the way home and hid in the basement until the driver, who'd traced her route back, rang the bell and asked my stunned parents if the young fair-haired girl he'd hit with his cab was hurt. My parents had to scout her out. I couldn't fathom why this incident seemed to be a source of shame for my sister. She didn't want attention. I didn't understand it, as her frisky, risk-taking kid sister, I was always looking to move into the spotlight.

We lived together for eleven years. She and I shared the fourth room of five in our third-floor apartment closed off from our parents' bedroom by curtain-covered french doors and our brother Willie's small back room by a plastic accordion door. Rosemarie (spelled as one word, she always pointed out) and I slept together in a double bed, shared the same metal clothes closet, a single chest of drawers and desk. There was nothing I didn't know about my sister Rosemarie who was nine years older than I and served as a chief role-model for what I had yet to experience as a young girl growing up on the streets of Bushwick.

A good part of my youth was spent inspecting her every possession when she was out of the house. Most titillating of all was examining the contents of her underwear drawer, stuffed with a treasure trove of slippery panties, strappy garter and sanitary belts, lacey slips and padded bras all effused with the sweet scents of dusting powder and cologne. She had no idea I tried them on, parading around in front of my mother's bedroom mirror, tinged with the dual excitement and terror that someone might walk in on me.

I tried on the sheer kerchiefs she used to wrap around her pin-curled head, half moon-style, with ends hanging down in back. I twirled in her petticoats and coarse felt flare skirts and wore her high heels, dragging scratch marks across the floor. I fastened Rosemarie's jingly charm bracelet around my wrist and emptied the contents of her two pocketbooks onto our bed, fingering each item: a comb, hankie, lipstick, bobby pin, as if it were my own. The only possession of hers I never touched was — her frosted, wing-tipped eye-glasses — something I knew, even as such a young age, would work against me.

When Rosemarie was in the house and either in the bathroom or downstairs visiting with Gram, I'd sneak into her plump blue wallet, dump out her change and count it along with the few bills inserted lengthwise. Thumbing through the bulbous stack of high school graduation photos of her friends, I'd find autographed pictures of her fan-crazed heart-throb Johnny Rae and of course, of her one and only boy-friend, Steve.

What the two of us shared without disdain for each others' territorial rights was a pine three-draw desk that stood opposite our double bed. She stocked it regularly — first as a student in the secretarial track at Bushwick High School, then as a highly-prized secretary for a vice-president at J.C. Penny's — with fresh blotters, crisp steno pads, typing correction liquid, manila envelopes and folders, message pads, red and blue ball-point pens all of which I was allowed to use freely. Also on that desk were the new technological wonders Rosemarie brought into our lower middle-class lives, a three-speed RCA Victrola and a grey-green Royal manual typewriter.

During the day, when my sister was at school or work, I'd take off her precious Johnny Rae's "Little White Cloud That Cried," and Frankie Lane's "Mule Train," and put on my own "Little Red Hen" and "The Magic Flute." Listening to the familiar repetitiveness of the musical cadences, I simultaneously hammered out key strokes — f-r-f — f-v-f — f-t-f — f-b-f — my eyes focused on the long, red, typewriter drill book I'd borrowed from the public library.

Because of our age difference, my sister and I usually saw each other when we woke up in the mornings or at night when she came to bed. Since my bedtime was a good deal earlier than hers, she often tip-toed into our room at a late hour. Feigning sleep, I'd watch her undress illuminated by streetlight slicing through the venetian blinds.

On one night, she jolted me awake, running from the hall bathroom through my parents' bedroom she catapulted onto our bed and screamed that she'd seen a mouse. Waking all three households, my hysterical sister looked as though she would have crawled into a mouse-hole herself when everyone convened on the third-floor landing and tittered at her overreaction to a helpless little Mickey. Another night, it was I who scared her silly while I was sleepwalking. The next morning I heard her complain to my parents that I'd gotten up in the middle of the night and made a racket jiggling the belts in our metal clothes closet and what if I were to sleepwalk into the kitchen and grab a knife and stab her to death?

My father told her she must have been dreaming.

She never understood too, that on one lazy summer morning in the double bed we shared, I was only trying to see what the next sequence of cartoon characters looked like on her pajama bottoms when I pulled a piece of the fabric out of the crack of her behind. It was quite innocent, my lying by her side contemplating her back with the little doggie on her pajamas jumping, skating, flying . . and wham—she turned around and smacked me but good. Called me a dirty little pervert and yelled for Mom.

My sister often "told" on me when she felt my mother should know I was doing something wrong. That gave her inordinate power over me, which I hated. Like the time I told Agatha about girls getting periods and stupid Agatha went home crying to her mother. Agatha's sister Rosalie just happened to be my sister's friend too, and word got back that I was spreading the "wrong kind of information." Another time when my sister worked at Nickel's Five and Dime along with my friend Cathy's mom, she discovered I was leaving school everyday and ditching my bagged lunch to eat at Cathy's house. I always had a lot of explaining to do once my mother found out, but I soon learned squealing worked both ways.

Because my mother had a job from the time I entered second grade, I was always being watched by someone in the household. When I was very young it was usually Grandma or Aunt Bea, but as I moved into my upper elementary school years, my mother increasingly left me in the care of my sister. "Take Beatrice with you," soon became my sister's misfortune when she went with Steve to Rockaway Playland, or for a hotdog at Nathan's on Cross Bay Boulevard or just hanging out on someone's stoop. All her friends knew me as the tag-along-cute-little-sister, which was in complete juxtaposition to my sister's own sentiments about my having to stick to her like glue. That's because I snitched on her too, telling my mom when she smoked a cigarette or stole away with Steve when she wasn't supposed to.

Sharing the same bedroom and having to take me everywhere may have been incentives for my sister to marry at such an early age. She was nineteen when she and Steve became engaged, twenty when they got married. I watched all the pre-nuptial fuss with guarded skepticism as my mother brought a hope chest into our bedroom and methodically filled it with linens and bedding she and my father bought on their Sunday treks across the Williamsburg Bridge to Delancey Street. Thanks to my father's intimate connections, a bridal shower was held at Charlie's Bar & Grill. Throughout the planning stages, I took it all in . . . a honeymoon at Mount Airy Lodge in a room with a heart-shaped tub . . . getting the license, the dress, the rings. . . not quite sure of what my role was in all of it.

It took me by surprise, when she announced I'd be a junior bridesmaid in her bridal party, bestowing on me the honor of walking down the aisle first, along with my cousin Joseph. I never dreamed she'd say yes when I offered to belt-out my own boisterous rendition of Pat Boone's "April Love" for her April 20th wedding, but she did, and I sang my heart out with the full and complete affirmation that despite the vast difference in our ages, our bond as sisters was strong.

I was happy to see the newlyweds take off in one of Steve's demolition derby cars, tin cans bouncing behind, to start a new life together. Of course, there was a motive. For nearly a year, I'd been eagerly anticipating what it would be like to have my own room, with my very own closet, and chest of drawers, desk and a bed all to myself. Finally, I would have the most prized possession in all of our three family household—privacy—something I realized even my sister would never have now that she was married. But a scant two weeks after fully occupying my own space, I was bored. Seeing it filled with my own hum-drum possessions paled compared to the clandestine discovery of unknown treasures hidden away in dark corners and the thrill of uncovering forbidden secrets.

Pondering this disappointing turn of events while tipped perilously backward on my desk chair, mindlessly tossing a Spaldeen in the air, I missed a catch and lurched forward. The ball bounced into Willie's room and rolled under his bed. Following to retrieve it, I noticed a large grey cardboard box labeled "letters." I got up ever so gently and closed the plastic door behind me.

UNTO THE SON

Because she was religious to the point of being saintly, I'm certain my mother-in-law would have been overjoyed had one of her sons become a priest. On the flip-side, my mother felt doomsday had arrived when my brother told her he had such intentions.

The whole time my parents, sister and I made our bi-weekly pilgrimage from Brooklyn to the meandering roads of Long Island's Smithtown, I kept my nose pressed to the back window of my Dad's rumbling green and white Chevrolet. I wanted to be the first to spot the bull, a giant green-mottled, well-hung statue that signaled our need to turn left onto the country lane that would take us up the hill to St. Anthony's Postulate.

As we neared the entrance where a chalk-white version of the Catholic Seminary's namesake welcomed us, I'd stick my head over the front seat to see if my mother had already started crying. She wept a lot the few months since my brother Willie announced he wanted to become a priest. I didn't understand what all the fuss was about—I was five, he at eighteen, had just graduated from high school—I hadn't yet begun my religious instruction, all I knew was my mother was heartbroken over my brother's abrupt absence in her life.

Rosemarie and I always felt Mama favored Willie over us. We used to confront her with "you love him best," convinced that his being her firstborn child and only son made him more special than the two of us girls. Her tiresome show of emotion then, over her sons' entering the brotherhood was something we pooh-poohed as a bit overdone.

For me, the excitement of driving out to the Postulate had nothing to do with my brother. As soon as Daddy parked the car on the dusty edge of the acres-wide sanctuary, I scurried off to entertain the other seminarians who'd encircle me with attention and laughter during my precocious rendition of "On the Good Ship Lollipop." My sister, at fourteen, wasn't allowed to be so frivolous, and sadly I thought, had to endure the boredom of the adult group she was quickly becoming a part of which included not only my parents but my aunts, grandmother, and close family friends who customarily followed us in a caravan of cars every other Sunday. Arranging themselves on a ring of benches, this adoring group formed a protective circle around my black-robed brother. Speaking in sober low tones, they looked up to the still-teenaged family idol as if he were Christ himself.

When it was time to leave, sure as anything my mother's eyes would redden. By the time we drove past the Smithtown bull, she could hardly contain the full-blown sobs that seemed to spill out involuntarily. My sister and I would look at each other, and roll our eyes heavenward.

There was a brief period of respite for the beleaguered woman when Willie decided, after six months of harsh deprivation and strict observances, not to take the vows of poverty, chastity and obedience afterall. But Mama barely had a chance to breath in and out before a second crisis erupted. Without discussing it with anyone in the family, her adored son signed up for a four-year stint in the U.S. Air Force. His first assignment would be Korea where a war was raging. This caused yet another torrent of heart-breaking tears.

My brother was a quiet guy, hardly completed a sentence, but when he did speak, what he said surely made a profound impact on the rest of us.

Until I turned ten I rarely saw the 5'10", dark-haired phantom. And when I did, our encounters involved my being scolded for leaving the cover off of the toothpaste or burning the toast. Who was this Willie who rarely inhabited our house and yet had such power over me?

I was so jealous of my brother then. He was the only member of our family with his own room and he hardly ever used it. It was the smallest though best room in house because it was the last of the three bedrooms in our railroad flat, and didn't have to be walked through by other family members. My childish curiosity drew me to this room just beyond the one my sister and I shared, probably because my mother kept it off limits, making it a virtual shrine in anticipation of my brother's sudden return.

When no one was home, I'd inhabit the room as if it were my own. Looking out the window to be sure the coast was clear, I'd inspect everything on his desk and the contents of all its drawers. What impressed me most was my brother's collection of jazz albums by Stan Kenton, Dizzie Gillespie, unfamiliar names I'd never heard of. This wasn't rock'n'roll, a subject I knew about, but jazz, in my home, my territory, what was it all about? I switched my sister's RCA Victrola from 45 rpm to 78 one day and listened to all of three minutes of someone called Benny Goodman before my Aunt Bea came stomping up the stairs to see who was playing my brother's sacred records.

Mama put a lock on Willie's door after that causing me to resent him even more. But, probably taking a cue from my mother's sappy behavior, I worshiped his attention too.

One day in second grade while waiting on line to re-enter P.S. 75 after recess, I saw this fellow with a wild colored satin jacket beckoning me to the schoolyard fence. It was Willie, on a furlough from Korea wearing a dragon jacket emblazoned with a wild tiger, so unlike the genteel person inside it. I ran to him and he twirled me round in a big circle, my friends hovered nearby, admiring my brother, MY brother. Or was it his jacket?

On another of Willie's furloughs, I thought I was dreaming when he invited me out to dinner, just the two of us. I'm positive he never asked Rosemarie out to dinner. Maybe it was easier to take me because I was the little sister, fourteen years younger, whereas my sister and he were five years apart. Wearing his informal khakis, the well-built crew-cut serviceman held tightly onto my hand as we crossed the streets en route to the dimly lit Chinese restaurant on Broadway. The combination dinners we ordered were quite ordinary, egg-drop soup, chow mein, fried rice and an eggroll, but what was extraordinary was the two-way conversation that took place above the table. I have no idea what it was we talked about, but I do remember my talking to him and he talking to me — providing us with a brief glimpse into each other's widely divergent lives.

By the time Willie's commitment to the U.S. government neared its end, we all held our breath to see what his next move would be. I don't know where he plucked it from, but pharmacy was what he chose to study when the GI bill guaranteed his way through four years of college. So at age 23, Willie finally came home to live full-time at 140 Grove Street.

From that point on, our whole three-family house turned into a mausoleum. "Shhh . . . Willie's studying," the three judges warned anyone who dared utter a word above a whisper, as once again, my charmed brother held an exalted position in our family, if not the whole block, as the first person to go to college.

Dad, who had been pretty much in the background regarding my brother's impulsive career choices—probably out of relief they didn't cost him any money—suddenly made it a point to teach Willie how to drive. During the day while my father was at work my brother was allowed to drive our dad's new green Chevy Bel Air 4-door sedan back and forth to St. John's University. Funny, but not really, our father never made that same effort with Rosemarie or me.

Willie's presence in our household put a major crimp on my life in two ways: the basement was off-limits and our food had to be prepared differently.

Having become the serious student, Willie staked-out our warm, cozy, furnace-belching basement, as his private study-hall. That meant I couldn't go down there after school with my friends to play records and dance. Mean as it may seem, I enjoyed the hoopla when a mouse had my big brother scurrying in fear, two steps at a time, up to our third floor apartment. I felt more sorry for Willie another time when, studying through the night, he fell asleep on a chair with one leg tucked under his body. The leg went numb to the point that he had to drag himself up the basement steps, gimpy-style, and needed to wear a brace for a number of weeks until the circulation returned to his deadened limb.

What really irked me about Willie was his aversion to cheese. That meant we had to cook a portion of most meals specially "for Willie" without it. A major blow to an Italian household—no ricotta in ravioli, no mozzarella in lasagna, no parmesan in meatballs—not even cheese on pizza—and worse than that, my father worked as a shipping clerk for

Lily Lake Cheese Company from which he always brought home hearty slabs of Meunster and Provolone! It was free, so my father was compelled to take it even though my brother retched at the sight and smell of cheese in our Frigidaire.

Thank God Willie got married right after college, to a beautiful, petite woman, well-dressed, a stunner, not at all what we expected of him considering his bizarre track record for picking things.

But it wasn't the wife my brother eventually chose, or his jazz collection or studying for the priesthood that influenced me the most about my oldest sibling.

When I graduated from high school, my seemingly wise and frugal father advised me to "go to work as a secretary like your sister, meet a nice young businessman and get married."

"No Daddy, I told him with a conviction and confidence I never knew I had, "I'm going to college like my brother."

Finally, it was his turn to cry.

A ROSE AND HER THORNY ISSUES

Much fuss was made when my husband, children and I all went to Italy to visit my mother-in-law's relatives. There was no such excitement about my extended family, most of whom lived on this side of the ocean, but then it might have been different had Nonna Rosa still been alive.

Family lore has it that my paternal grandmother was pregnant with thirteen children, but I only knew seven of them; the others having died at birth or of tragic illnesses early in their lives. The six boys and one girl who survived were all given colorful identities by their brother (my father) and I grew up knowing all them tinged by his warped and wicked sense of humor.

My dad characterized two of his brothers as puppets because they were dominated by their wives, another was a gambler and the fourth, a barfly. The only one I never heard a disparaging word about was my father's eldest brother, the tailor, and that may have been purely out of respect for his position in the pecking order, but more than likely, it was because he passed away when I was too young to pick up any snide remarks about this particular uncle's personality flaws.

My father's sister, too, received her share of ridicule by marrying a vaudevillian hoofer half her size. This small man put my aunt on a pedestal, treated her like royalty, which rankled my dad to no end since her previous role in Nonna Rosa's household was that of Cinderella, scrubbing and washing and tending to a houseful of rough-necked boys.

Much of what drove my father into fits of jealously had to have been rooted in the competitiveness of sleeping three-to-a-bed in a cramped cold water flat, of fighting for the last meatball, waiting one's turn for a weekly bath in the kitchen tub, and lining up outside in the dead of winter to use the outhouse.

None of his siblings were educated past eighth grade, which was the norm for children of Italian immigrants who grew up during the Depression. Even while attending school, the boys hustled work as assistants to truckers and shop-keepers, making their childhoods all the more brief. My father found a job helping the ice-man haul giant blocks of ice up the rickety stairs of tenement buildings for a nickel or a dime. With hardly any place to stash his precious coins among nine pairs of nosy eyes inside his tight dwelling, he managed to find a secure spot out in the hall, under a rug in a communal space that lay between his and another family's front doors.

Or so he thought. Bounding up the stairs one day after school, my young father was startled to discover his mother had rolled-up the rug to mop the hall floor. Not a coin was in sight. They stared at each other, he knowing that she found his hard-earned savings, she incensed that he didn't share it with the family, as was expected of all the boys with their earnings, and the matter was dropped without another word being uttered.

My father was afraid of his mother but, aside from the turkey incident, Nonna Rosa didn't seem threatening to me at all. She died when I was in second grade so I knew her for only a short time, and what impressed me most was her great girth. A well-rounded mid-section, gelatinous bulging arms and triple chins intermingle in my memory with the floury smell in her kitchen of fresh pasta being made or biscotti cooling from the oven. She kept a huge tin of homemade cookies in her parlor cupboard and I was one of a gaggle of grandchildren who dipped into it freely, as if it were there for us alone.

Her husband, Grandpa Vito died the week I was born so I have no recollection of him. Only the photos of a portly man, still clearly smaller than his wife, dressed in a three-piece suit with watch fob and pocket hanky, white hair and handlebar-mustache groomed for the camera, provide a reflection of what he looked like. Surprisingly, his Sicilian skin was light.

Nonna Rosa's was too. Her skin was even fairer, framed by wisps of pale custard hair wrapped in a loose bun with large V-shaped hairpins. She was the epitome of what Grandmas should be, her flabby outstretched arms, welcoming, encircling. A significant gap marred her yellow-toothed smile, but her skin was like a soft magnet that drew me in for a kiss or a hug or an embraceable squeeze. What I couldn't do was understand her, since she spoke only Italian, but in the universal language of the young and old, I knew she loved me by the twinkle in her eye whenever I burst through her door.

I loved Nonna Rosa too, but going to the bathroom in her apartment on Gates and Knickerbocker Avenues was the awfullest thing. It shouldn't have been called a bathroom at all since there was no bath or sink in it. You couldn't have even called it a toilet because situated as it was in the hallway between two opposite apartments, it resembled more of a closet with a wood bench that had a big hole cut into it. I always felt that one day my small Raggedy-Ann body, legs dangling off the floor, would fall down that hole like the drunkard in Roseann's basement, and no one would know where I'd disappeared to. A chain had to be pulled from the water tank overhead to flush the contents of what went into the hole, and a putrid stench permeating the small space was a deterrent for anyone to linger. I tried with all my might, never to have to use that bathroom, but if I did, I'd hold my nose and count to twenty, which made the act of balancing and elimination all the more perilous.

During those early years when my uncles and aunt were newly wed and raising families, they settled within walking distance to Nonna Rosa's apartment. They'd shop for her, help give her a bath and visit every Sunday after church, but amongst themselves, the brothers and sister and their spouses reserved the end of the work week to visit each other.

When they came to our house on Friday or Saturday nights, my mother put out some chips and pretzels, and my dad would line up bottles of soda, whiskey, beer, blackberry brandy along with a bucket of ice on the dining room table. I'd play with the Maraschino Cherries and stirrers in my highball-glassful of ginger-ale, and sit listening to the adult conversation. Being the next to youngest in a large family, the adults naturally fawned over me. That encouraged me to entertain them with ditties and childish patter which they reacted to with knee-slapping claps and guffawing laughs. It made me feel good when they'd ask "are you bringing BeBe?" the next time my mom and dad were expected to visit, and my parents always obliged.

I especially loved being able to walk a few blocks on warm summer nights to drop-in on my aunts and uncles, and mingle with them outside in their front gates or stoops while dipping into a freshly bought lemon-ice from the open-air window at Circo's Pastry Shop. But I was seeing it all through a child's innocent looking glass.

As I grew older, I realized there was always dissension within my father's clan. At any given time throughout their adults lives at least two of the brothers and sisters weren't talking to each other. And my dad, I'm sorry to admit, was one of the chief instigators. I'm sure they had no clue, but nick-names were his specialty.

His sister was "Mrs. Maud" not only because she looked like the well-coiffed, elegantly dressed Bea Arthur in the show by that name, but because, he was convinced, she had a habit of being superior just like that TV character. He turned livid whenever they dined out together and she'd make a point of dipping her silverware in the water glass and wiping it with her napkin to make sure it was clean. Though he was clearly steaming over what he considered her insulting behavior, he kept it bottled up, never expressed it until he returned home — then we had to hear about "Mrs. Maud" for weeks afterward.

The name "Rumpot" was reserved for his younger brother who was known to frequent bars. If the bell rang unexpectedly, my dad would run to the window to see if it was him. If it was, he'd make a mad dash to hide all the liquor in the house before answering the door. He doesn't want to see me, he just wants to empty my bottle of Four Roses," my father later spewed to my mother and me.

He had kind words for his two other brothers, but didn't take kindly to their wives, who according to my father, "wore the pants" in their households. He giggled at this, as if his brothers were sissies.

I suspect they had their own names for my dad. For sure, he deserved it. Sadly, the hurt feelings and touchy affronts that zinged back and forth among some of my father's siblings caused tit-for-tat spats that grew into one or the other's not being on speaking-terms for years on end.

Fortunately for me they all liked my mom, and I grew up in a household filled with her siblings, a place where the silent-treatment would never have lasted beyond a single intake of breath.

A CHRISTMAS LEGACY

The one time I saw my mother-in-law at a loss in the kitchen was when she was handed a knife and encouraged to cut designs in the dough for the traditional holiday fig cakes my family makes every Christmas.

The warm, sweet smell of pastry dough wafting through the cellar door on a cold blustery early December day always beckoned us from our outdoor play on Grove Street in the 1950's.

Tumbling through the wrought iron gate and down the basement steps, my cousin Joseph and I would follow our noses to the heat-radiated fragrance of gas-fired ovens. Next to them stood Grandma Beatrice wiping her flour-covered hands on a corner of her soft cloth apron. She was all of five feet tall, her hair wound into a classic Italian bun.

Grandma always underwent a personality change during the weeks before Christmas. A normally shy and unassuming woman, she was suddenly transformed into the hustling, bubbling directress of baking operations at our three story Brooklyn walk-up.

Like my recollection of "The Little Red Hen," Grandma bought the flour, rolled the dough, mixed the fillings and prepared the pans all by herself. But unlike the selfish hen who would not share her fresh baked bread with the lazy barnyard animals, Grandma delighted in watching her three grown daughters and their offspring participate in decorating the delicate Christmas pastries they made every year and test the results.

One of my brother's favorites was the "cassatedda", a moon-shaped pastry filled with a mixture of ricotta and bits of chocolate then dusted with powdered sugar. In a rare moment of impishness, Grandma always filled one "cassatedda" with cotton. That provided a source of amusement for us kids as we'd watch with gleeful anticipation the expressions on the faces of everyone who bit into one. My brother Willie usually spent hours poking at each ricotta-filled pastry to find the one with the most give.

Grandma always set aside another day for making "pignolate" — long strips of rolled dough cut into small dice, then deep fried, drained on split brown paper bags and glued together with honey and almonds.

But the "pignolate" and "cassatedde" were mere precursors to the main event which drew every family member into the basement — even the men, and especially the children — for the making and baking of the fig-filled cuccitate.

Since the age of sixteen when Grandma emigrated to the States in 1906, she continued to make the cuccitate that was a family tradition in her beloved Sicilian hometown of Santa Margherita Belice. There, during the month before Christmas, neighbors and family members would gather at various households and using the plentiful figs that were indigenous to the region, bake trunk-loads of cookies that would carry them through the winter months. Today, distant relatives in Santa Margherita Belice claim that this practice has long been considered "antica" or old fashioned, and no one goes through the trouble of baking the "cuccitate" anymore.

But the branch of our family on this side of the ocean knew only of Grandma's determination. On the morning of its preparation, she laboriously rolled the dough for the "cuccitate" with a large wooden dowl and passed dried figs through a cast-iron meat grinder. Afterwards, in-laws, uncles, cousins and grandchildren sat around her table with knives poised for carving the names of new grandnieces, their favorite sports team, hearts, crosses and even Christmas trees into the pastry. The finished carvings were laid onto large black iron trays, brushed with egg-wash, sprinkled with non-pareils and baked to a golden color. Uncle Joe, the official taste-tester, always stole a cuccitata from the first batch and invariably declared it was the best we'd ever made.

It came as a terrible shock for all of us when in 1976 at the age of 84, Grandma was felled by a stroke that left her paralyzed on one side. When Christmas approached the following year, we all noticed she was not really up to dealing with the festivities of the season.

I waited until two weeks before Christmas before taking it upon myself to visit Grandma and bring up the tender subject of baking the cuccitate. By then my mother, her eldest daughter, had passed away and I was pregnant with my third child. I'd suddenly become aware of my role linking past and future generations and felt an urgent need to preserve the few family traditions that remained.

With her mouth stretched back to one side, Grandma reluctantly translated to me the three recipes that, over the years, she'd painstakingly penciled into a 10-cent marbled copybook. Stopping every so often, she'd interject in a manner that was self-defeating, "c'e troppo lavoro—this is too much work."

And in the beginning it was. No matter how I tried, I could not get the dough to adhere into the elastic smoothness necessary for rolling it out.

Two short hours before my entire family was to arrive— my sister bearing 5 lbs. of prepared figs—I cursed my heroic attempt to become the family martyr and was about to call everyone and admit my defeat when to my wonder, the mealy little marbles of dough began to blend into a pliable texture ready to be rolled and filled, cut and baked.

We made 130 fig cakes that year and on Christmas Day, when Grandma bit into one of them, a crooked smile spread across her face and the old sparkle came briefly back into her eyes.

Though she died two years later, the tradition lives on. It's been 40 years since we've made the cuccitate without our family matriarch, and it still takes more than one person to do the job. My grandmother's great-grandchildren Tommy and Gerard set up the pasta machine which has taken the place of Grandma's rolling pin. Aunt Bea oiled the same old wooden cutting board that used to sit atop the rickety basement table and Aunt Min, who ceremoniously distributed the sharp knives that are used once a year, specifically for this task, have both since passed.

My sister Rosemarie, who lovingly prepared the figs every year, died too. As did her daughter, Donna, who took up the task in her absence. The teamwork and conspiratorial delight we took in accomplishing this together continues to weigh heavily on my desire and ability to carry on.

But I do, and have slowly passed the torch to the next generation, which has rolled up its sleeves and taken over. My sister's offspring now prepare the fourteen pounds of figs, still laboriously with an old-fashioned meat-grinder. And my daughter Paula makes the ten pounds of dough— amazingly, the cuccitate come out perfectly consistent and sweet every time.

Somehow Grandma Beatrice imbued her namesake with the same legacy that was passed on to her. For while our hands may work the dough, surely it is her spirit that holds it together.

THE THREE BEARS

Over the years, I'd observed practically every facet of my in-law's family dynamic, and could pretty much gauge what it was like for my husband to grow up in a household that remained intact for such a long time. For him, there was no reciprocal looking glass. By the time he and I met, the number of family members living in my house had dwindled to two.

To outsiders, my immediate family likely resembled the classic story of The Three Bears, my father being the breadwinning Papa Bear, my mom the aproned Mama Bear, and me, of course, the irrepressibly adorable Baby Bear. But, if I were to write a children's tale of my own, I'd portray our characters more realistically: dad would be the oft-feared grizzly, mom a gentle panda, and me, a big-eyed koala observing all the goings on from my omnipresent perch.

Hearing my parents' wedding song, the popular 1930's ballad, "Let Me Call You Sweetheart," played over and over again on the Victrola, I was puzzled as to how its romantic lyrics referred to them. Even to my very young and innocent ears, the words didn't quite reflect my impression of their sentiments toward each other. It could be I missed the lovey-dovey part of their relationship, having arrived a good fifteen years into their marriage when annoying patterns of behavior had already begun to frazzle their connubial bliss. Or maybe living alone with them for a ten year stretch after my brother and sister married, caused me to witness two very different individuals sharing the same space.

I know why my mother was attracted to my dad. He was one of six rollicking and raucously fun-loving sons of a neighboring "paesano", all of them handsome and considered "good catches" for eligible young women eager to walk down the aisle. His name was Ignatius, but most people called him by his middle name, James, or Jimmy or simply, Jim. Dressed in his finest, the 5'10" darkly handsome Jim cut a suave image from his black-banded gray fedora and Charlie Chaplin-like mustache right down to the tips of his spiffy white spats. Plus, he owned a car during the Depression years, thanks to a steady job as a truck driver protected by the Teamsters' Union, an organization more respected than God himself by my father and his brothers who were members of the cheese, butter and egg locals.

Family lore has it that Nonna Rosa, fed up with her playboy sons, suggested to my father it was time to settle down. She encouraged him to call on the nice daughter of a paesano who lived a few blocks away.

"I asked your grandfather if I could take your mother out and he told me one of her sisters had to go along as chaperone. I told him to forget it and sure enough, the next day the old man came knocking on my door to say it was okay for me to take your mother out alone," my father bragged years later.

From what I gathered, my notoriously strict Grandpa Giacomo, aka Jack, had met his match in my strong-willed father. I wondered why my mom didn't realize if my dad really cared, he would have accepted the chaperone.

That thought was probably overshadowed by an opportunity for the blossoming young eighteen-year-old to escape her Mussolini-like father. Grandpa Jack was so ornery, Grandma Beatrice was forced to smuggle in sweets for her children to savor behind the dark cloak of the cellar door, at the supreme risk of being caught with powdered sugar on their faces and scolded for wasting the meager wages her husband earned laying railroad tracks. Fortunately, I was only five when Grandpa Jack died, so Grandma's house never held any fear for me. All I remember of the old man was his sitting in a straight-backed chair smoking a pipe near a window while every few minutes pitching up a guttural wad of phlegm into a spittoon.

My mom, Leonarda, or Lena as everyone knew her, was the oldest of Grandpa Jack's three daughters. There were two boys too, but I never got to know them — one, a baby, lost his breath after my mother, a toddler herself at the time, slammed a door on his tiny fingers; the other succumbed to a rheumatic heart at a young age.

Left with only three daughters, to save face and maintain his self-respecting reputation among the neighborhood paesani, the family patriarch was expected to marry his eldest off first.

I can't really say what physical attributes attracted Jim from Gates Avenue to Lena from Himrod Street. She was ordinarily plain with a medium build, her face, framed by dark hair and eyes, was remarkable only for its slightly hooked nose. Though her sisters, Bea and Minnie tell me how chic she was in her heyday — dressing fashionably in chiffon chemises, velvet flapper helmets and python shoes — old photographs I have show her posed wearing sturdy lace-ups, a shirtwaist dress and apologetic half smile. There was no question that Aunt Bea was prettier and other young ladies in their circle of friends sexier, but Lena's personality was easy-going and compliant and I tend to think Jim, or at least his mother, knew he needed that in a woman.

After a 1932 football-style wedding, named for the salami, ham and Provalone sandwiches thrown like footballs across rows of long plastic-covered tables, the newlyweds set off across the Williamsburg Bridge to spend a one-night honeymoon at the Commodore Hotel in Manhattan. My brother Willie was born a year later, my sister Rosemarie four years after that. By the time I came along in 1946, my parents seemed more opposite than alike.

He drank beer and hung out most Friday nights at the corner bar; she smoked half-a-pack of cigarettes a day and visited her mom on Friday nights so Aunt Minnie could color her hair. He was boisterously loud and easily angered, she was meek, her fits of giddiness legendary, especially at the end of a busy workweek, when she was tired from her job at the sweater factory and any silly remark set her into jags of laughter that ended in tears. He was generous with money — leaving me a quarter for lunch when he'd read the note I left him in the top basket of the coffeepot every morning — but never went out of his way to drive me to school or to a friend's house, so I could avoid the threatening neighborhood gangs.

She was not frugal, but cost-conscious, dragging me to E.J. Kleins or Alexanders on bargain-hunting expeditions for an Easter suit or graduation dress, never paying full-price. She also kept a tight rein on my boyfriends and was pretty much in charge of where I was allowed to go. "Don't ever come home pregnant," was the extent of our "girl-talk" about sex.

Dad was a jokester who laughed heartily at his own antics and wisecracks. He'd pose on his knees for the camera, his head resting on a sawed off tree trunk with one of his brothers hoisting an axe over him. But there was the hell of frozen silence to pay if someone teased him back. He was easily insulted, hated to be made a fool of, and like an elephant, remembered slights against him, turning them into grudges that for years caused him to be "not on speaking terms," at one time or another with practically everyone he'd built a relationship with.

This always caused problems with my mom because she was well-liked. Her popularity as a favorite aunt and sister-in-law, often conflicted with his enemies list, sparking jealous tirades that turned my father into a tempestuous two-year old. Lena's constant position was one of placating Jim, and apologizing to others because of him — a diplomatic skill she possibly picked up from her own long-suffering mother.

"Oh, what a hard worker he was," Uncle Sal once told me about his older brother Jim. My mom must have known that, to put up with his combustible temperament.

She was content to take a back seat from the action, whether it be dancing at weddings — my father always did the peabody with Aunt Minnie—or at family gatherings where my dad would take center stage performing his signature routine of a rooster crowing, causing a dog to bark, waking up a baby, with all the accompanying cacophony. Instead, she found enjoyment in simple, solitary pursuits, making her own living room drapes or cooking my father his favorite dish of Sauerbrauten. Sometimes she did venture out with Aunt Minnie to a Broadway play or the Harvest Moon Ball, but those outings were few and far between.

What my father and mother did do as a couple with me always tagging along, was food shop every Friday night (my father's payday) for a week's supply of groceries that filled exactly four bagfuls at Bohack's. Saturday nights the three of us visited aunts and uncles who lived within a ten-block radius.

Basically all of our activities revolved around their adult lives. I always went along with them, but they seldom made an effort to come with me. I begged them to attend the school and church plays I regularly performed in, or awards' ceremonies for which I was expected to receive a badge or certificate of merit. They both shied away from that kind of involvement, making me feel as if I was imposing on them, but viewing it backward, their immigrant upbringing and lack of education may have caused them to be intimidated.

My mother did give in, eventually attending a few of my performances, mainly because Aunt Minnie made my costumes and they went together to view her handiwork under the bright lights, but my dad never attended anything—not even a teacher's conference—ever, not once.

I tended to overlook these slights in the summers when school ended and the three of us drove up to the Catskill Mountains for a week-long stay at a paesano's bungalow called, of all things, "The Brooklyn House." I was shocked and felt utterly left out one summer when they abruptly changed plans and conspired to go away as a couple to celebrate their 25th wedding anniversary.

What could they possibly be doing at the tony Fountainbleu Hotel on Collins Avenue in Miami Beach for eight days without me? Me, the glue, I surely thought, that held them together.

But when they returned, all tanned, with bagsful of souvenirs and black and white snapshots recording their happy stay, I saw something in their eyes that I'd never seen before — the flicker of an old flame perhaps, rekindled, and a signal for me these two "sweethearts" shared something I wasn't privy to.

It was then I descended from my lofty lair, wandered out beyond the reaches of my den-like existence and turned my attention to the Gates Avenue Gang.

PART IV—BICE

Il proverbio: "chi va piano, va sano e va lontano" (he who goes slowly, goes safely and far).

BIG CITY CAMPUS

According to my mother-in-law, a woman's place was in the home where her duties were to cook, wash, feed and nurture her family. Since she conquered those tasks with such ease and to such a superior degree, I'm certain she'd have made mincemeat out of her professors had she gone to college.

My first impression of the New York City college I was about to enter in 1964 was that I had somehow arrived at the wrong address. Glancing up at the grassless, 17-story building that loomed before me on Park Avenue and 68th Street, I thought I'd made a huge mistake. I could have kicked myself for not applying, as most of my friends did, to Brooklyn or Queens College where the sprawling grounds provided a real campus environment. The reason I didn't was driven by a memory from early childhood.

I was in the sixth grade when two of my girlfriends were singled out to take the entrance examination for Hunter Junior High School because they had high I.Q.'s. I didn't even know what an I.Q. was, and no one ever told me that it was possible to attend school outside my own Brooklyn neighborhood. I felt sabotaged. Distancing myself from these two girls, I studied them from afar, trying desperately to discover what it was that made them so special, so different from me.

Six years later, when Hunter was listed among the five

city-colleges that I could apply to in my senior year of high school, there was no question that I would make it my only choice. Being accepted there automatically settled the score of my purloined youth, from then on I merely followed the script as it unfolded.

At first, I was woefully disillusioned there were no fraternity houses, beer-mixers or rousing football games like those my friends in the outer boroughs enjoyed. But in time I discovered much of my college experience would occur during the two and three hour breaks between classes, when I began to inch out onto the concrete campus and explore the city around me.

One of my very first outings during freshman year was to the Central Park Zoo where I was immediately initiated into the sorority of big city life by of all things, a pigeon! Plop! Back to school I ran with warm smelly goo dribbling down my neck and tears of humiliation pouring down my cheeks.

Another venture out was more subdued. I took shelter on a rainy day in a nearby movie-house with a female classmate with whom I'd made casual acquaintance. Ingmar Bergman's "Persona" was featured. Knowing nothing of Bergman or his style, I managed to sit through quite a number of uncomfortably suggestive scenes involving two women. Vulnerable to its message and rather inexperienced in this genre, I went back to my next class less talkative, more grown-up and afraid to look my companion in the eye.

As days turned into weeks, I moved further from my 68th Street outpost. The museums in particular, piqued my interest and I began to use them like textbooks.

What struck me like thunder was my first encounter with "real" art. It was Rembrandt's painting of "Aristotle Contemplating the Bust of Homer," importantly displayed inside the main entrance of the Metropolitan Museum. The painting drew me in like a religious experience. I bought a postcard depicting that painting and began to keep a collection of such mementos to verify having seen the works of great masters with my naked eyes.

On an ordinary day it wasn't unusual for me to walk up to St. Patrick's Cathedral where the Cardinal himself might be saying mass or slip into any number of airline offices near Rockefeller Center to browse through travel brochures of faraway places.

Frequently I'd come across picketers or a demonstration and would stop to listen. Once a motorcade passed in front of me, its diplomatic flags flapping briskly in the wind. I'm sure I glimpsed the back of President Johnson's head in one of those cars on that day.

In winter, I found a good place to take refuge was in the cozy and very elegant lobby of the Plaza Hotel, where I'd sit for a while on a high-backed, leather chair. In warmer months I'd head up to Central Park's Sheep Meadow for gym class. It was the closest thing to an athletic field that our school had access to, and if it weren't for the dog-droppings, we could actually imagine that we were on a real college campus.

Our field hockey team practiced there too, and more than once a dog would take off after our ball and we'd have to bully it all over again. Walking back to Hunter after a game, we'd coyly flip our short skirts in front of the boys' soccer team, eliciting a welcome string of wolf-whistles.

With hockey sticks slung over our shoulders, taxis screeched, vendors hawked their wares and a pungent mix of sewers and subways wafted through sidewalk gratings as we dodged garbage cans and baby carriages back to the venerable halls of scholarly pursuit.

Once back at Hunter, I never quite knew what to expect. A noted politician running for office might be shaking hands in the main lobby or a blond-bombshell actress would be filming a commercial in the cafeteria — and during her break she'd drink the same machine-acid coffee as the rest of us.

The sound of clamoring bells resounding in rapid succession, invariably signaled yet another 1960's bomb scare.

I sought refuge during those evacuations some ten blocks away at Bloomingdale's. From there I could always catch my first train ride home—one of three that I took every day from Manhattan to the outskirts of Queens. The cars of the IRT, BMT and what I'd come to affectionately call the "depression line" served as my study hall. When philosophy and economics texts no longer held my interest, I would slowly lift my eyes and shift my attention to the people around me.

Discreetly placing a book between us, I watched how they flopped into their seats as the train lurched predictably forward. I observed their sometimes rough, sometimes delicate features and movements: the expressions on their weary faces as they yawned—their lolling heads dipping deeper and deeper onto their chests as they drifted into sleep. Though most subway riders seemed to be bored, they were never boring to me. I studied them as intently as I did the Rembrandt painting.

On some lucky nights, I'd be spared the long rain ride home when fellow classmates invited me to stay overnight. Their homes never seemed to be in the elegant vicinity of the Park Avenue school, but rather in Alphabet City or Spanish Harlem.

On one of those nights spent in the city, I found myself ice-skating in Central Park's Wollman Rink with a handsome young fellow who claimed to be an actor. There I was, Sonja Henie, dancing round and around in the arms of my famous leading man: at every turn we'd glance at each other, then back again to the panoramic view of the ice-crystal city at night.

During summer sessions, I'd return to old reliable Central Park where free concerts were given on the rolling expanse of great lawn. A most memorable evening was spent there with a dandy music major, spread out on a blanket under the starry sky imbibing a bottle of bubbly rosé.

By the time junior year rolled around, I'd come to feel quite comfortable in the city's familiar surroundings and even chose to remain there when classes ended. During mid-semesters and summer vacations I joined the legitimate workforce as an office-temp, filling in wherever my rudimentary typing and clerical skills were needed, uptown one day and back downtown the next, taking whatever jobs were assigned to me in advertising or motion picture companies, fashion houses; for publishers and banks. On my lunch hours I'd browse through book stores, art galleries and novelty shops; stop at fountains, sit on a park bench, or watch tug boats chug up the East River.

Truth to tell, there were some instances that were frightening, like the time I was solicited by a "John," in front of the old Coliseum, yet others, such as coming upon a circus parade on Fifth Avenue, or turning a corner and bumping into Jackie O., were positively exhilarating.

Each day on the brink of something new and exciting — that's how I remember my college years, not in a closed setting but experiencing real-life, at its very worst and very best, at a big city campus on the diamond-glistening sidewalks of New York.

FAIRY TALES DO COME TRUE

If my mother-in-law had the old neighborhood crone read the future, she probably would have put the "malocchio' (evil eye) on any girl, Sicilian or otherwise, who came within three feet of her 20 year-old son. Lucky for me, my mother had supernatural powers of her own.

Being a girl, the three foot tall ragmop doll called "Waltzing Matilda" should have been mine, but like most other store-bought toys I coveted when I was a child, it belonged to my cousin Joseph. The most I could expect to own were jacks or a yoyo bought for a nickel or a dime from the corner candy store, my pint-sized cohort was always luckier. Even though it was "sissyish" for the pre-schooler to slip his feet into the elastic bands of Matilda's stuffed feet and dance to Aunt Bea's melodious version of "Gonna dance with the dolly with the hole in the stocking, knees keep a knockin', toes keep a rockin," I envied him, and longed to be the one rocking in his tiny shoes.

Having just entered kindergarten myself, I was newly exposed to the thrills of rhythm and movement in P.S. 75's musty basement where circles of five year olds swiftly progressed from Ring Around the Rosy to the Farmer in the Dell. In that same basement through the early elementary grades we squared off for the Virginia Reel, linked arms for the Troika and joined upturned hands to dance the Hora. By the fifth grade we were counting to the beat of ballroom classics—the basic box step, the waltz, and cha-cha.

My mom asked me to teach her the cha-cha for my sister's upcoming wedding. It was a new craze she'd seen performed at her beloved Harvest Moon Ball, a dance contest she attended every year at Madison Square Garden with my Aunt Minnie, who was the dancing sister . . . Aunt Bea was the singing sister: my mom was the least lively of the bunch.

Teaching my totally compliant mother to dance after she came home from work at five o'clock every day was the most cherished memory I have of our mother-daughter bond. She wholly trusted me, let me lead, I wasn't used to that. Whenever I danced the fast-paced Lindy with my sister Rosemarie, she always insisted on leading. Now, finally I was in command and I liked the heady feeling of being in this new role.

Following the beat from the scratchy record player, my mother and I repeatedly stepped into the steady rhythm of one-two-cha-cha-cha, with me prodding her backward, forward, sideways and back. We stopped, started over, giggled so much that we had to pee, but tantamount to it all was the warm sensation of holding each other arm in arm. Like a shadow, she flowed with me around the dining room table, past the kitchen and out into the hall, inevitably causing someone downstairs to ask what all the commotion was about.

My mother did dance the cha-cha at my sister's wedding, to the surprise of everyone. Even Grandma Beatrice's traditional toe-stepping to the tarantella paled in comparison to her daughter's impressive moves on the dance floor. For once, my mother stood out among her siblings and shone like the star that she was. And I felt pride in helping her accomplish that.

What I wasn't proud of was entering Halsey Junior High School with a learning deficit. Luckily, I didn't sign my name when my new 7th grade social studies teacher gave us a quiz on the 13 original colonies. He chose my list to read aloud, no doubt because it included the Philippines, Jakarta and Istanbul. The ensuing laughter infuriated me. I knew at once it wasn't my fault, it was Miss Reid's because all we ever did in her 6th grade class was dance.

In an effort to transfuse our veins with the green blood of her beloved Erin, the spinster teacher dressed in demure plaid skirts and man-tailored blouses, taught us to stand erect with hands at our sides, heads stiff as we performed the hop-hop-down-hop-one-two-three-four of the Irish Jig. Those times when we weren't "in Dublin's fair city, crying cockles and mussels, alive-alive-o-oh" we were allowed to move the desks to the side of the classroom and dance to the 45 recordings of the 50's popular rock-and-roll tunes. Truly, the only skills I picked up in sixth grade took place in my legs which, in addition to the jig, learned how to do the hop, stroll and buggedy-shoo.

My dance repertoire grew to another dimension at Halsey where the white and black students each occupied half of the gymnasium at weekly after school dances. We took turns playing our favorite tunes on the record player and in those pre-stereo, pre-speaker times, blasted the volume as loud as we could.

While our side danced the bouncier teeny-bop twist and pony to the strains of Fabian and "cutesy" Brenda Lee, I studied the slower-seductive movements of the black dancers on the other end of the gym, marveling at the way they sashayed to "the slop" and pressed against each other for the steamier "grind" to James Brown or the Isley Brothers.

I never noticed what the boys wore, but the girls shopped along Broadway all week for that one outfit that would prompt the boys to ask them to dance. All the rage then were short, white middy blouses that hung loosely from the shoulders and flared out—both the black girls and white girls wore them as tops, but the choice of skirts was glaringly different. Our group favored brightly colored button-down culottes or wrap-arounds, the black girls, whom even we white girls considered more adult, wore tight, black skirts that generated heat with every pulse of their Motown beat.

On Friday and Saturday nights most of the Gates Avenue Gang hand-carried their little square boxes of records to one another's homes where the dancing to selections of the latest hit songs took place until it was time to leave. I never had my own records, probably because I never had the money to buy them.

By ninth grade, many of us were paired off—Linda and Steve, Cathy and Pete, me and Frankie C.—and we began to favor the slower ballads, so we could dance close, or sit on someone's basement couch with the lights dimmed, and make-out.

My dancing days dwindled during high school when Grandma sold our house and I had to change schools. Lacking friends in a new neighborhood, I concentrated on my studies. Skipping the entire Joan Baez hippie scene, I moved straight into college mixers with the Beachboys, where, slurping Sinapore-Slings, I'd wait along the sidelines for some college Joe to ask me to jump onto the dance floor to do the "swim."

By the time I was a college junior I was meeting real men at sophisticated clubs. Graduating to Johnny Walker Black Label, I started hanging out with a group of working girls and tagged along with them on Friday and Saturday nights to clubs with cover-charges featuring star entertainers. Wearing high heels with upswept hair, I mamboed and merengued to the drumbeat of Tito Puente and slow-danced to Frank Sinatra Jr.'s in-person renditions of his father's famous torch songs.

It was to one of these nightspots my friends encouraged me to go two months after my mother died. I'd just started as an elementary school teacher, and was struggling with my mother's request that I mourn her for a year after she succumbed to colon cancer. I didn't think it was appropriate to wear black in the classroom for a whole year, so I'd already broken that promise.

How could I break another? It was a lonely two-person apartment I came back to at three o'clock every day, my father headed straight to the corner bar after dinner most every night. Filled with guilt and remorse, I reluctantly agreed to go with my friends to D's Den on Queens Boulevard a week before my 22nd birthday, but I warned them not to expect me to dance.

But they did. And that left me alone nursing a drink at the bar. "Do you always wear one earring?" someone asked over my shoulder. Instinctively, I reached up, both earrings were fastened securely in place. When I turned to look at the body attached to the sweet-talking prankster, my insides caved-in. The sleek, sharply dressed, six-footer was a drop-dead dreamboat.

Before I had a chance to respond, the band struck up a Perez-Prado tune. "Like to cha-cha?" he asked. From somewhere out of the blue I felt my mother give me the signal to go ahead.

We were married two years later.

THE HEART

While the deeply religious "Donna Maria" knelt in church week after week, confessing her sins to an Italian-speaking priest, her younger son was out toying with the truth.

He told me he was an economics professor when we met at a local singles club in 1968. It was as if a thousand strings were pulled together in one tight knot. He was everything I was looking for in a guy—besides his good looks and engaging personality, he was smart... and Italian, a dream come true. Bracing myself against the bar at D's Den, I dipped my index finger into my scotch and soda and made the sign of the cross.

The blond-haired, blue-eyed construction worker I was dating off and on at the time couldn't understand why I didn't want to see him again. He was fun to be with, we bowled and went to the movies, but beyond that our mutual interests hit a brick wall. I was a school teacher studying for my Master's Degree and always assumed our relationship was going to be short-lived, something to fill the time until I met Mr. Right.

"I'm seeing a professor," I admitted, thinking that somehow he would get the full picture. He didn't and was crushed. I felt selfish and guilty to be so suddenly detached, but no matter how hard he tried to convince me we had a future together, I only heard the rapid beat of my love-struck heart.

My newfound beau and I talked on the phone and met at the club for six months before he actually asked me out on an official date. I couldn't tell which way the wind was blowing, but decided to hang on with all my might.

When he finally did ask me out, it was to see a Broadway production of George M. Cohan with dinner afterwards at the pricey Athena East, first-class treatment I thought, which was what I always longed for in a mature relationship with a sophisticated man.

When I told my family I was seeing a professor, I sensed a newfound deference from my father and aunts, my sister and brother, no doubt for my ability to attract someone so learned.

Finally, they were showing me the respect I always knew I deserved.

My professor took me to the opera, albeit, a small production of Pagliacci in Nyack, New York where the audience sat on folding chairs in a church basement auditorium. We visited museums and he recited to me long verses of poetry written by his very brother, who he told me was also a professor even more esteemed than he. I was dazzled by how different he was from the other boys in my hood and quickly fell into a deep romantic stupor. He came to my house while my dad was out wooing other women and cooked a heart-shaped meatloaf, I, in turn, played the Jimmy Rosselli albums he bought me over and over again. He gave me a cameo bracelet, handmade by an old Italian jeweler, and I bought him a woolen scarf. We called each other, bubbling with giddiness from adjacent phone booths on the streets of Manhattan, and sat side-by-side in the spray of the fountain near the Brasserie were we ate breakfast at the break of dawn.

Four months into our deepening relationship he told me he had a confession to make. Clearly, he was struggling with what he had to say. My eye began to twitch. I thought he'd tell me he was married or reveal something even more horrible, that he was an ex-convict! Instead, he acknowledged quite sheepishly that he wasn't a professor after all, but had recently graduated from a college in downtown Brooklyn near Junior's Restaurant on Fulton Street in an accelerated two and a half year program. Painstakingly, he disclosed how he was a year and a half younger than I, and that's why it took him so long to ask me out because he needed to borrow a car and that he still slept in the same room with his brother in his parents' Bronx apartment.

"Wha????" I sat dumbfounded for a long while on my living room couch digesting all that I'd been told, trying not to feel like a fool as I bore down on the hard truth that the person with his arm nervously draped over my shoulder no longer fit the image of the one I'd fallen in love with.

Evidently he'd been trapped and I'd been caught by a line he'd always used in a playful little ruse he and his buddies dreamed up to attract and impress young women when they went club-hopping. They all had lines, he said, it was an inside joke among them to say they were yachtsmen or real-estate moguls, but he had no idea it would ever backfire on him in a relationship that turned serious at this young point in his life — a relationship like the one ours was fast becoming.

How gullible or desperate must I have been not to recognize my enchanting professor wasn't even old enough to be a professor??? How could I possibly be so naive? He certainly looked older to me. This little drama had upset the applecart in my brain, and I found myself having to backtrack and reassess my options.

It didn't take long for me to come to the conclusion that it was too late to pull back — I was already unequivocally and impossibly besotted with the man-boy behind the image.

Telling my family was harder for him than it was for me, but he managed to win them over with his warm generous nature and wit.

That's when we all became acquainted with Mikey Heart. It was a nick-name the neighborhood cronies called my former-professor on Arthur Avenue in the Bronx, a tag, I learned, that accurately reflected his expansiveness for helping others. He gained this reputation by rescuing his contemporaries when they came home drunk in the early morning hours or flunked out of school and he smoothed things over with their mothers. As a result, the grateful women fed him at their kitchen tables and encouraged their wayward sons to be more like Mikey Heart.

Making the voyage across the bridge from Queens to visit my new boyfriend in his Bronx neighborhood during those early courtship days was like traveling to China, though China was surely closer because everyone knew all you had to do was dig to get there. My family didn't know a soul who lived in the Bronx, or Staten Island for that matter. Unless we were going to Manhattan, there was never a reason for any of us to cross a bridge. The outer boroughs were so alien to my father he said I had rocks in my head the first time I innocently asked for a lift to the other "B" borough. There was no alternative but to navigate from Queens through Brooklyn and Manhattan to the Bronx on four elevated and underground trains.

And I began to learn about that borough through the slant of Mike's experiences, meeting characters as diverse as street corner Dion-types singing four-part harmonies, brothers from the Catholic school briskly wisking by in their long-skirted robes, wiseguys sitting at outdoor cafes drinking espresso and old-timers playing bocce in the local park.

What I discovered was his Fordham neighborhood was as dear to him as my beloved Bushwick was to me, only he was still lucky to be living in a community where he could casually greet classmates he'd known since first grade. With time, I got to know some of them too, because Mike took me to their homes and introduced me to their mothers as they made fresh pesto sauce or homemade raviolis, and later attended their weddings.

Besides walking the main streets of the tightly-woven Italian 187th Street and Arthur Avenue enclave with its pork stores, pastry-shops, bread bakeries and salumerias, we also strolled up and down the more commercial Fordham Road with the behemoth Alexanders and Loehman's department stores anchored at each end of the busy thoroughfare. Sometimes, we ventured further to see the Botanical Gardens where hosiery and slips hanging from trees on early Sunday mornings bespoke the victories of Saturday night conquests. Mostly, I was struck by the number of double-parked cars in that neighborhood.

On Sundays while my new beau's mother was preparing the requisite family dinner after Mass, we'd steal over to Fordham University to sit on a park bench and watch other young lovers sprawled on blankets across its lush lawn. I listened with complete absorption as he described how he and his friends used to search for horse-chestnuts that fell from the many trees on that campus, soaked them in a secret home-made brew, nailed them to strings and staged competitions to see whose horse-chestnut was the hardest and strongest in a swinging duel.

We moved not far from that campus when we married, to the more rarified tree-lined streets of Pelham Parkway. I had a hard time convincing my family it was worth crossing the bridge to visit me from Queens and Long Island, but eventually they made the journey.

Though my new husband had completed the course work for a Ph.D. before we were married, he stopped short of writing a thesis and chose instead to forge his way into the business world and no one — not even his strong-willed mother who wanted both her sons to be called "dottore" — was able to stop him from doing so.

"Be-ya-tree-chay," she said conspiratorially pulling me into her tiny bedroom, "you're the woman of the house, you should insist my son to go back to school for his Ph.D." But I was never quite as convincing as she in that arena. Try as I might, I could never stop what my dear husband started.

With time, I came to realize it was his plan to achieve his mother's goal through a different door anyway.

He actually did become a professor and would become awarded an honorary Ph.D. some forty years later. Sadly, his mother passed away shortly before that took place. I can see now, the grand plan was there all along, simply lying dormant until Mike was ready to make his moves.

In the end, I married my professor, "Donna Maria's" dream for her youngest son came true and Mikey Heart wasn't a liar after all.

READING, WRITING AND ROOM 308

She never admitted it because it just wasn't her style, but deep down inside I think my mother-in-law liked the idea that if her daughter-in-law had to have a career, it would be as a school teacher. In her uncompromising value system, education ranked second to Godliness.

Of all the teachers who traveled daily to and from public school 213 in Brooklyn's East New York in 1968, I was the only one to commute by bus. It's not just that I didn't have a car that was mortifying to me my very first year as an elementary school teacher, but I was the only member of the entire staff who didn't even know how to drive. I was four months shy of turning 22.

My fifth graders were the first to pick up on this vulnerability in their newly minted teacher.

"Why ain't you got no car, Miz Cicio," taunted Gabriel Del Toro, the leader I was soon to learn, of The Little Red Devils, a gang of 10- and 11-year-old boys most of whom were assigned to room 308 — my class. The stocky boy's eyes twinkled and his mouth smirked when he asked me this as the class lined-up for dismissal one day.

Fortunately, I was saved by the bell, but it was only a temporary reprieve.

Unlike the other teachers who eased into different, private worlds the minute they slid into the front seats of their cars at 3 o'clock, I had to schlepp my belongings to the corner bus stop and wait, sometimes up to a half-hour in scorching, blustery and foot-soaking weather for my passage out of one of Brooklyn's toughest neighborhoods and into the genteel, tree-lined streets of Ridgewood, Queens.

The youngsters who waited for me to come out the school's side exit and walked along with me to the bus stop were usually the ones, like Gabriel, who needed the most attention.

"Miz Cicio, is that a real leather jacket you wearin'?" he provoked in his usual nettlesome way. It wasn't. The smart-alecky 11 year old knew the difference between real and fake—a "Red Devils" trademark with threatening pitchfork and horns imprinted on the back of his own Hell's Angels-style jacket was probably embossed on the real thing.

Gabriel and his threatening band of young renegades may not have been in one of the most progressive classes in the fifth grade, but they were by far, the sharpest to understand lessons that weren't taught in text books. My role in teaching them to divide fractions and remember how to use new vocabulary words was a challenge beyond anything I'd learned as an eager, pumped-up save-the-world student teacher.

But I had my limits and Gabriel bumped up against them one too many times when a new student from Haiti came back from lunch period one day in tears. The Little Red Devils, he sniffled, forced him to eat dog doo in the street. Immediately I searched for the gang's ring-leader, grabbed his hand firmly and dragged him down to the Principal's office where his grandmother, his sole guardian, was summoned. She wrung her hands and looking woefully at the beatific face of her grandson, mumbled she didn't know what to do with him.

That was judgment day for Gabriel—his last in my class before he was transferred into that of a more seasoned teacher. What stayed with me though, was his heraldic name, which introduced me to the piousness of the Latino culture, as did other students I taught in the three years I was at P.S. 213. There was Lourdes, Baltazar and the hardest of all for me to verbalize—Jesus. Out of habit, my own Catholic upbringing had me piously bowing my head every time I called on him in class.

It took a long time for me to learn to pronounce Jesus with an "h" instead of a Jesus with a "j" and just when I got the hang of it with Javier, Juan and Jose, a new boy by the name of Jorge came into the class. His name was pronounced with a soft "j."

Other names impressed me in a different way, conjuring up Rorshak-like images that I couldn't shake throughout the school year. In my mind's quirky eye, Lorna Patterson became the cookie, Lorna Doone; slim, shy Birtha Slaughter reminded me of a freshly killed chicken and Edsel Myrie was the vision of a low-slung, wing-tipped sedan.

Most of their surnames were deceivingly mundane. The very ordinary "Little" was paired with Carthawa and Cleveland came before, not after Thomas as one would expect. Just as confusing to me every year when I first opened my attendance book was to figure out if Rhodell was a student's first name or last. It was his first.

Besides names, I was exposed to other cultural eye-openers when I visited some of my students' homes.

One of them was Jacques Landers yet another "j" name though spelled the French way. I'd written a note to his parents about his inattentiveness in just about every subject, and arranged to discuss it with them in person. Greeting me from his disheveled sick bed, Mr. Landers through rheumy eyes and coughing up spittle, apologized for his son's poor report card. The air was filled with the stench of urine, I tried not to take in deep breaths. Next to the bed stood Jacques, staring idly into the space of the stinking world he lived in, and I suddenly realized this poor youngster had greater things to worry about than memorizing the times tables.

I paid an unannounced visit to Ronnie Eply's house because of his frequent absences. When I arrived at the address listed in my record book, there were no names on any of the bells. A shaky staircase loomed ahead, rising into darkness. Outside on the stoop, I asked some men if they knew which apartment the Eply family lived in: they shook their heads. I left like a deflated balloon and had an even longer wait for the bus that day, but word must have somehow gotten back to Ronnie because he showed up in class the rest of that week.

Only once in my three years of teaching was I invited to a student's home for dinner. Mrs. Davidson, little Nicky's mother, asked me over for a roast beef dinner, which I ate with gusto until roaches suddenly surfaced and fanned out across the wall above the stove directly behind where Mr. and Mrs. Davidson were sitting. Nicky, who sat next to me, saw them too, and watched, with mouth full and big eyes in anticipation of my reaction. Outwardly I made none, inwardly my stomach lurched. As soon as Mrs. Davidson divulged the purpose of the special dinner, to ask me to tutor her little Nicky at lunchtime, I quickly agreed and begged off to catch my bus.

Riding home that night, I shook out the contents of my book bag and purse to be sure none of the little critters were hitching a ride with me.

I already had experience with roaches in my classroom. They scooted around by the sink in the back, near the art supplies, a part of the room I tried to avoid for that very reason, and I was constantly calling the janitor in to spray. I made a fuss about the roaches in the teacher's lunchroom and was surprised that many of my colleagues didn't seem as disturbed as I was. The male teachers especially, seemed blasé, but then, most of them were treading water, writing hum-drum assignments on the blackboard while engrossed in the newspaper — waiting for the Viet Nam draft to end so they wouldn't have to teach.

I, meanwhile, dealt with the likes of Cleavon Roberts whose hyperactivity was so disruptive to the rest of the class, I sought help from the school psychologist. When I later learned that the reason Cleavon had calmed to the point of being lethargic was due to medication prescribed specifically to quell his unbridled rambunctiousness, I felt responsible and extremely guilty for the sudden change in his youthful demeanor.

I felt the same wrenching tug in my stomach when I learned that chubby little Velma Osborne couldn't concentrate in class not because of her worn, patched up eyeglasses, which is what I thought, but because she'd recently been raped by her uncle at home in her bathroom.

During lessons on health I'd pick up other bits and pieces of my students' lives that explained why they came to school with their hair matted — because there was no hot water — why their teeth were beginning to rot at such an early age — they ate potato chips for breakfast — and why so many of them had perennially runny noses — they owned no umbrellas or boots.

Our relationship was symbiotic — I taught them reading, spelling, mathematics, science and social studies and they taught me about the struggle for survival with the odds often stacked against them, about humility, happiness and forgiveness. Watching them laugh and sing, sashay or express anger in the purest form of honest expression I've ever encountered, taught me more about life than I could ever impart to them.

And though I moved on, got married, had my own children and learned to drive, I still carry the imprints of those long-ago faces in my memory. I look for them in the adult strangers I pass walking down the street. I search for them on buses, the subways, in newspapers and on TV. Sometimes I think I've spied Edsel playing pro-basketball at Madison Square Garden or Birtha drawing blood from a patient in a health clinic. All 110 of them from one fifth and two third grade classes must be close to fifty now, probably married or living with someone, maybe working or on welfare, some may be in jail or even have died, though I pray hard to Jesus with a "j" that's not so.

Knowing their tenuous beginnings were balanced on such fragile foundations, I worry about the paths they've taken. I'm afraid that somehow Cleavon was steered into a life of drugs, or that cherubic Velma will continue to be sexually abused. I wonder if Nicky Davidson finally learned how to read and whether or not the roast beef his mother prepared for me actually paid off.

For some reason, the only person I don't fret over is Gabriel Del Toro. He always struck me as someone who could take care of himself.

WHEN DADDY AND I GOT MARRIED

Even my mother-in-law, who was usually forgiving when it came to men, was sympathetic when she witnessed my chagrin at the rigamarole my father put me through while planning my wedding.

It was supposed to be the happiest day of my life, I was a bride, finally . . . at 24, the last of my girlfriends to get married. It should have been a crowning moment straight out of Disney but the sentimental fantasy of walking down the aisle arm-in-arm with my teary-eyed dad played out more like a gut-wrenching soap-opera.

I had good reason to worry, Daddy was getting married exactly two weeks after me to a woman he'd met through a computer dating club. As Yogi Berra would say, it was deja-vu all over again. I went for my invitations and he went for his; I picked a catering hall and so did he; limos, flowers, rings, photographer, he shadowed me in every way and though I'm sure he wasn't aware of it, overshadowed every joy that was supposed to be connected to my own long-awaited fairy tale marriage.

My emotions swung from elation to sadness to utter embarrassment. I was elated because I'd hit pay-dirt with Mike. I was bringing home a fine young man: respectful, educated, with impeccable manners—any other father-of-the bride would have given his eye-teeth for his daughter to bring home such a prize, but mine was too blinded by his own love-life to celebrate my good fortune. I was sad because I wasn't being treated like "daddy's little girl" as I felt was my birthright, and became increasingly embarrassed by the over-the-top way my supposedly "adult" father was handling himself as a single man.

Like a horse let out at the starting gate, he began dating women less than two months after my mother died, and even though I'd met and started to date Mike during that period, I couldn't understand or accept my father's almost immediate interest in other women. I needed to decompress and thought he did too. My mother's death was so fresh on my mind, I was experiencing a powerful withdrawal from her and the aftereffects of the all-consuming two-year struggle she waged against a horribly wasting colon cancer. I ached for her. Pitied her. Was in pain because I could no longer share these thoughts with her and hide behind her maternal shield.

While in this frame of mind, my father really knocked the wind out of me when the very first person he asked on a date—even before the dirt settled on her sister's grave, was my Aunt Minnie!

Sitting across from the man I'd lived with forever but hardly knew, on a couch that still had my mother's warm imprint, I asked what on earth possessed him to do such a thing? He cried, said he was lonely, didn't know anybody else. I glared back, flared my nostrils, bared my teeth to show my resentment and for a while at least, he seemed chastened.

A month later, his continued self-indulgence gave me no choice but to run away from home. He'd called my mother's best friend Mary, the only person we knew who was widowed and remarried, and she set him up with a blind date. I could feel my mother turn face-down and hide in her freshly seeded grave... first her sister, then her best friend. My tolerance level overflowed with rage: for myself, because I alone had to live with my dad and the pressures he placed on me, and for my mom—whose 35 year commitment to a not-so-easy to get along with husband was rather quickly being swept into oblivion. It didn't feel right, so I walked out, slammed the door behind me, a signal that this battle had turned into a war.

I took the bus to my brother's apartment and spent a tear-filled weekend trying to decide what my next move would be. I was being consumed with my father's foibles at a time when I should have been comforted by him. Because I was his youngest child, I guess I expected a paternal kindness, a gentle bonding between us as survivors instead of a steady focus on him and his needs. Three months without a partner may have seemed like a lifetime for my father, but I was still trying to transition myself from being my mother's caregiver to that of my father's "auxilliary-wife," in a diminishing household of two.

I was tortured too, with guilt, because of my own budding love affair. Should I have been holding my father to different standards than my own? Were we equals in this game of love? I would never have given up my own promising relationship with Mike; so why should I expect my father to give up his own pursuit of love for me? Was I being selfish?

Through a series of phone calls to family and friends, Mike hunted me down at my brother's place, his growing concern for my well-being and coddling affection were ironically paternal. I'd just turned 22, was in my first year of teaching, had been earning a salary as well as, I felt, my stripes as an adult, and decided the best thing to do was move out on my own. My brother and sister were right behind me — they called my dad, told him we'd all be there the following night to pick up my belongings and to be prepared to give Mama's wedding and 25th-anniversary rings to me, as she'd bequeathed in her will.

My 63 year-old father sat stolidly, on a straight backed chair in the dining room, with arms folded across his chest, and watched as I emptied my and my mother's closets of clothes. When it came time to handover the rings, he whimpered like a lost puppy, apologized for the upset he was causing in my life and begged me not to desert him. "Don't go, I need you," he said. Not "I love you." My resolve cracked. I unpacked but kept and hid my mother's rings.

The next thing I knew, my repentant father had enrolled in a computer dating service and his little black book expanded exponentially. By then, I'd resigned myself to his desperate need for female companionship, and was almost ready to accept its inevitability. Almost. The calls started to come into our kitchen wall-phone all hours of the day and night, from Sally and Margie and Tess and because my father was hard-of-hearing, I wound up answering them most of the time. "Hi, is Jimmy there?" "Jim home?" "Is this James Cicio's house?" they asked in unnervingly gay voices. All I could do was grind my teeth and hand over the phone.

Hearing Jimmy-boy coo "honey" and "baby" and "doll" on the receiving end of a mouthpiece my mom scrubbed with ammonia on a weekly basis made me want to rinse my father's mouth out with soap.

If he needed to have women in his life, why couldn't he have been more discreet? Both of us would have fared better if I didn't have my nose and eyes and ears rubbed in these intimate love-fests. I was so angry and disillusioned that my childhood hero — my cohort on jaunts to Far Rockaway and Valley Stream State Park . . . a man who caught mice, killed bugs with his bare hands, drove an eight-wheeled semi and chased thieves from the cheese factory where he worked — suddenly espoused the maturity of a prepubescent teen.

For the first time in my life, I began to wear a bathrobe around the house, suddenly uncomfortable with the thought that my own father was looking at women's bodies with a newfound sensual eye. I hoped he would take the hint and do the same. He didn't. What he did do night after night was walk out the door uncharacteristically spiffed-up and doused with cologne, leaving behind a trail of awkwardness in our small Queens apartment.

At no time was that more glaringly apparent than one summer night, when we'd both gone out on respective dates. Mike and I arrived back at the apartment after an early movie and were snuggling on the living room couch when we heard laughter and a key turn in the door. I jumped up, ran to the hall and found myself looking into the frozen headlights of my father's eyes — clearly neither of us expected each other to be there.

Even more astonishing was the blond, high-heeled woman whose hand my father held behind him. We exchanged awkward introductions before my father whisked his ladyfriend off on a personal tour of the rest of the five room flat. I sat back on the couch nestled in Mike's arm, and listened with utmost reserve to my father's show-and-tell through my mother's belongings.

I observed everything I could about the woman in the short five minutes it took for her to tour the apartment. She struck me as the antithesis of my mom. She seemed gutsy and outspoken, mama was comely and placid. It was street-smart vs. homebody, with street-smart in the stretch. They looked as different as night and day too—mama had dark hair, wore modest dresses and sturdy shoes—this woman was short but loomed large with a tall behive hairdo, tight dress and pointy spiked-heels. Listening to those heels click-clack on my mother's highly waxed linoleum floor, I wondered whether this latest "lady-friend" would ever be able to hang my father's drawers on the clothesline without losing her balance and toppling out the second-story window.

It was a ridiculous thought, but one that held the serious weight of what was to follow.

Soon, he was dating this woman exclusively. She might have been a good woman, but I was uncomfortable in her presence basically because of my father's track record for making me feel that way. He went ga-ga over his lady-love—bought her a fur stole, diamond earrings, everything my mother waited years for, but this new woman acquired in record-splitting time. I found my father falling under her besotted spell and since I'd placed myself in the adversarial position of immortalizing my mother, in saint-like fashion, it would be the rare person who could fill her shoes—especially someone who wore spiked-heels.

I was ill-at-ease with another woman in our house, worming her way into my father's life, corralling his attention, at a time when I wanted and needed it too. Of course, I would have been mortified if she knew I'd been secretly dipping into the eggplant parmesan she'd sent over regularly to win my father's (and perhaps my own) favor. It felt good to be nurtured.

But my dad once again blew the lid off any relationship I'd ever have with a woman of his the day we sat down to discuss my wedding plans. With his prior blessing if not shove in that direction, Mike and I had become engaged and planned to be wed a year later.

Problem was, my father and his new fiancé wanted to get married too, six months before we did.

"Where will you live?" I asked incredulously.

"Right here," he said matter-of-factly, his scheme already devised.

"But what about me?"

"You can stay here," he said pointing to the tiny bedroom I occupied, which was sealed off from his by a flimsy accordion door. If I could hear him snore through it, I certainly would be able to hear him making love.

"NO," I screamed, banging my fist down hard on the armrest of my mother's cerulian blue couch. "You're not getting married before me."

Lashing into him with the honed tines of a forked-tongue, I sought revenge where I knew it would hurt the most by pitting his poor, warped sense of judgment against that of his clearer-thinking lady love.

She'd been a widow for nine years; her mourning period was over. Plus, she waited for her last daughter to get married — which happened to take place just before this conversation — so why couldn't my father show the same respect for me???

Dribble, dribble. Sniff, sniff. Here comes the sob story.

"I don't know how much longer I have to live. Your mother was younger than me, I'm going to be next," he said genuinely frightened. I got off the couch, held his bawling head to my stomach and comforted him. I loved my dad. He did need me, but couldn't express it without falling apart. And I needed him too.

That only went so far. I managed to convince him to wait for me to get married first, but that concession was cancelled-out by his half-hearted offer to pay for my wedding. He needed tight control over the invitation list, he said, because of the double expense of having to pay for his own affair two weeks to the day after mine.

He was relieved, smiled almost, when I told him Mike and I would pay for, and by extension, control the details of our own wedding. I was hurt at how readily he agreed. My fairytale version would have had my daddy give me the full-blown wedding I deserved, if only for my mother's sake, while he would re-marry in a more subdued fashion.

That's what I was thinking when we walked, arm-in-arm down the aisle on my wedding day.

MADONNA OF THE POT

Growing up Italian-American in Brooklyn, I thought I knew everything there was to know about Italian food, but that was before I was introduced to the "Madonna of the Pot."

In our family, we ate spaghetti with meatballs on Sundays, lasagne on Christmas and Easter and crusty seeded "scalida" bread every night with dinner. What was absolutely unheard of in our middle class household was eating bread with pasta. It was as alien to my Sicilian-born grandmother as Chinese' serving bread with rice. That's why she reacted as if a bombshell hit her kitchen table the day I scooped tomato sauce onto a piece of bread.

"Where did you learn this?" she asked.

Her suspicions grew when I asked why we never drank wine. Beer and soda were the beverages of choice in our extended three-family household.

"Beatrice, what's happening to you?" my namesake asked as if the answer would rip her heart out.

Indeed, what happened was I had met the woman who would shape my culinary tastes in the years to come, my future mother-in-law. No wonder my grandma felt threatened, she was up against the "Madonna of the Pot," the most tenacious bearer of Italian cooking since Marco Polo introduced spaghetti into the Italian diet.

When we first started dating, Mike took me to his house every Sunday for dinner, a weekly ritual Italians from all regional backgrounds hold sacred. Initially I felt honored to be treated like a guest, but as I became a familiar fixture week after week within the four-person household — Mike, his mother, father and elder brother — I was subliminally recruited into the preparation phase of the meal. That's when I became a candidate for sainthood.

It was no coincidence my then 70-year-old, 5 foot, 155 pound mother-in-law's name was Maria, same as the Blessed Mother, queen of heaven and mother of all children. Mama Maria proved to be Regina of the cucina too, the mother of all cooks, and I, the only other woman in a house full of men, was to be the sole worshiper of her timeworn, pot-filled miracles.

For the first couple of months in her antiquated kitchen, I wasn't allowed to actually touch a cooking utensil — all I could do as an apprentice was stand aside and observe as the Apulian Queen of the city of San Marco in Lamis turned the barest of peasant fare into dishes that, some thirty years later, would quite remarkably be the most expensive items on the menus of upscale Italian restaurants.

But I didn't know the quality of what I was being exposed to then. All I knew was to be respectful and do what was expected of me if I wanted to land my man, which I did in earnest.

Knowing what is ingrained in every signorina's psyche from birth, the surest way to a man's heart is spelled, "m-a-n-g-i-a," I plotted to comply.

So on Sundays, I was tied up in a full-length apron and sent off to the clothes closet where a secret trove of jarred tomatoes stood lined up next to my brother-in-laws shoes. It was an epiphany for me to see these jars stacked in neat rows; until then I didn't know tomatoes for making the Sunday sauce came in anything but cans.

My mother-in-law, "mia suocera" in Italian, lifted each plum tomato out of the green prune juice bottles that she recycled for such purpose with individual reverence before splashing them down into a pot that would transform the drippy orbs into a bright red, thickly consistent gravy. Sometimes it was made alla marinara, other times with a meat base, steeped with fish, olives, eggplant or cacciatore-style.

My suocera-to-be was just as devoted to greens I'd never heard the likes of—broccoli rape, scarole, chickoria, arugola—each so bitter I recoiled at the taste. The water they were boiled in was even more bitter, but poured into Flintstone jelly glasses and consumed for "la salute", good health—this ablution was deemed holier than the greens themselves—nothing was wasted in my mother-in-law's house because it would be, in the name of the father, son and holy ghost, "un sacrilegio."

"Non mangio fagioli," I don't eat beans, I protested in the Italian of her Sammarchese dialect, the sole language she spoke and one she passed on to me through her perpetual incantations. Whenever she tried to push lentils or ceci or cannellini beans on me, urging to "prova, prova," try them, her first or second attempts always ended in a struggle of spilt beans. But in time, I began to acquire a taste for pasta con lenticchie and pasta e fagioli and paid close attention to how the beans were rinsed, soaked overnight and added along with a chopped potato, onion and garlic to a brodo or salsa rossa to enhance their flavor.

Her perspiration-inducing preparation of the thick gluey, yellow mound she called polenta seemed like a rite of penance. By itself, the cornmeal concoction was tasteless, and I couldn't understand why the poor old woman labored over the pot, stirring the slow-to-thicken mass for well up to half an hour, her face flushed crimson from the effort. No doubt my quite sweet and docile father-in-law sensed my lack of fervor for sampling the grainy blob, as he encouraged me to try a slice drizzled with red sauce, with "peperoni fritte", fried peppers, or roasted in a frying pan the next day, as a leftover, and I became a believer.

She made me eat flowers too. Zucchini flowers. While most of civilization buys the green cucumber-like zucchini at the vegetable market, my future mother-in-law sought out the pale yellow-tendriled blossoms the plant made. She dipped each lily-shaped flower into a mixture of flour, eggs and parmesan cheese, added salt and pepper and served them as an appetizer. "Mangia," she commanded — the most frequently used word in her vocabulary — and by this time, I knew the only way I could stop the sermonizing was to open my mouth.

But I had my limits. I wouldn't do so for tripe (the stomach lining of cows), capozzella (lamb's head) sanguinaccio (pig's blood) or the homemade preserved vegetables that I suspected were riddled with toxins, especially after I heard the lady across the street's husband died of botulism after eating his wife's jarred mushrooms. Always protesting that I was too stuffed to eat these highly prized delicacies during a meal, "La Madonna of the Pot" would give me a jar of pickled eggplant or peppers to take home. Religiously I made the sign-of-the-cross and dumped their contents into the garbage, returned the empty jars and told her they were "deliziosi" (prompting her to give me an even greater supply the next time I visited).

Another form of torture I had to endure was the "forte" — dried, spicy red pepper buried in every prepared dish or liberally sprinkled over one's dinner plate without consent — that sent me flying to the sink for a glass of water. Sometimes I doused the fire on my tongue with a glass of red wine poured from a gallon jug my future father-in-law kept under the table near his feet. It was my first introduction to wine of any sort and its acidic, ribald coarseness required a water chaser too.

It was as alien to me as the green sauce "Donna Maria" made out of basil with a mortar and pestle called pesto, the homemade potato pasta, she said was gnocchi and the fresh tomato and bread salad she referred to as panzanella. My Italian vocabulary was growing like grapevines in the heat of summer. Meanwhile, my dearly beloved and ordinarily placid grandmother, couldn't believe that, despite her own efforts to keep my Sicilian roots strong, I was being converted ever so slowly, into a Pugliese.

But then she'd never come up against the potent will of the "Madonna of the Pot" or the lure of budding love. Though the year-long journey started in my future mother-in-law's old-fashioned white-tiled kitchen with wood-painted cupboards, it ended at the altar which is where all Madonnas and those who worship them belong.

GREAT EXPECTATIONS

Seven months into my first pregnancy my in-laws, both of them all of 5 feet tall, showed up arm-in-arm at my back door right after dinner one night. I sensed it was a momentous occasion the minute they bypassed the kitchen and walked straight down the hall to our more formal living room where they perched themselves at the edge of the couch and sat stiffly at attention.

Quickly drying my hands with a dishtowel, I lumbered after them and eased my bulbous girth into a reclining chair. Pushing-off with my feet, I bobbed like a lifeboat on a rolling sea.

The conversation quickly turned to naming the baby. It was a subject I knew first-hand. Being a Beatrice, I'd long-since decided no child of mine was going to fall into the trap of being a mini-me or a mini-she or mini-he.

As soon as I learned I was pregnant, I went to the library to scout-out books on baby-naming. I didn't have to search far through their alphabetical lists for boy's names. I liked the ones that started with "a" — Andrew and Anthony were my favorites. For girls, I went all the way to "p" before falling onto a cache of all-American names to my liking — Patricia, Paula, Pamela, Penny — I adored them all.

My husband wasn't as focused as I was on this one aspect of childbirth. . . he was more willing to stick to tradition by naming our firstborn after one of his parents.

Rubbing my belly, the belly that held the blossoming fruit of our dual creation, I glared at him from the recliner.

I was afraid of offending my in-laws, but felt strongly that I needed to win this battle for my child's sake, so he or she could have an identity of its very own on the branch of a tradition-laden family tree. I stopped rocking and planted my swollen feet on terra firma.

" These are modern times," I said smiling to keep the mood light. "young people of our generation no longer follow the old ways."

After much squabbling over this in the days that followed, Mike and I eventually struck a truce. To appease his parents', a boy would be named Michael to preserve his father's lineage for yet another generation, and to appease me, a girl could have any "p" name I wanted.

As for what this newborn would look like when it made its debut, that vision already filled my dreams. Gender was never a factor, I had neither a clue or desire as to whether it would be a boy or girl. What I was sure of was, upon arrival, this baby would be olive-skinned, like my Sicilian side of the family, with dark curly hair, and so chubby he or she would look like a buddha. That vision burst the same day my water did — five weeks before my expected due date.

"Stop teasing me," my sister railed on the other end of the phone when I told her I'd started premature labor the very night the two of us booked a surprise 65th birthday party for our dad in a catering hall. I'd been dragging her in and out of the maternity sections of department stores for over two months looking for a dress to wear to that occasion. Nothing seemed to fit. I couldn't close the last three buttons on my maternity tops and was bursting through my yawning pants at the seams.

An x-ray in the hospital revealed why.

"Yep, just as I suspected," said the radiologist who held a black sheath of film against a fluorescent light. "Here are the two spines and it's a good thing for you both heads are pointed down in position."

"Two??? Both???" "Whaaaa???"

When it finally registered in my brain that I was about to give birth to twins, all I could think of was names. Michael was a given, but what other name would go with it if I had two boys? And how could I match another name to Paula's? Should they both begin with the same letter like Michael and Mark or Paula and Penny or should they be totally free of each other's identity?

My husband paced between the labor room and the waiting room where his parents' kept a vigil on their knees reciting the rosary in Italian for the whole 24-hour period preceding the actual births. Meanwhile, I struggled with contractions and various combinations of paired names.

I bounced the possibilities off my jittery spouse every time he poked his face through the curtained wall that surrounded my bed.

"If we name one boy after your father why don't we name the other one James after mine?"

He nixed that but offered his brother's name, Joseph, instead. I balked and the tit-for-tat went on. During my sister's periodic calls from the catering hall where my entire family was anxiously waiting to make an announcement of the double birth over the microphone, she relayed to me names my relatives were shouting at her into the phone.

The effort consumed me until it was time to deliver — then, as if two thousand-pound burdens were lifted from my birth canal — I remember hearing the celestial pronouncements spaced four minutes apart, first "it's a girl" and then "it's a boy."

The hospital rendered the name issue moot by referring to the firstborn as A-baby and the second, B-baby. The tiny three-pound infants weren't immediately identified by their chosen names because the hospital staff wasn't sure they were going to make it.

But while the fair-haired, light skinned, frail little twosome were hardly as robust as I'd pictured in my dreams, they had what it took to survive and thrive. As for their names, I managed to keep my in-laws happy and exercise a bit of my own free will by christening them Paula Marie and Michael Joseph.

In the end, I wasn't really surprised that the twins turned out to be a boy and a girl since throughout my pregnancy, I never had an inkling of what sex I was carrying. And I wasn't surprised three and a half years later when I became pregnant a second time, and was sure beyond a doubt, I'd be giving birth to a girl. I had the name all picked out — Pamela — it went well with Paula and just seemed to fit. When she arrived, with tumbling dark hair and fleshy folds on her arms and legs, this baby turned out to be the one in my dreams.

Forty-four years later, both Michael and Paula are married with their own children. I stayed out of the baby-naming business and eagerly anticipated the names they would pick out of the wind and attach to them: Alexa, Matthew, Julia, Sarah, Samantha, and only one Michael. I marvel at the progress made in just one generation and revel in the future of their individuality.

A TALE OF TWO PUPPIES

For a woman who professed a disdain for dogs, my mother-in-law slipped enough food under the table to feed mine, I may as well have served the whole meal on the floor.

"Aw, don't get a dog, Ma," whined my teenage daughter when I broached the subject with my family thirty years ago. A dog would interfere with our lives and create problems, she said.

Her twin brother who never agreed with his sister on anything, was quick to side with her. "We don't need a dog and if you get one don't expect ME to walk it!" My husband joined in. "They smell. . . they bark . . . and they bite." He grew up without a dog and had no desire to include one in his life now, he said in no uncertain terms.

Only my eight year old, whose big brown saucer-eyes brightened at the mention of a dog, liked the idea. She even promised to walk, feed and clean up after a brand new cuddly little puppy.

I felt the same way at her age. When I was eight I brought home a German Shepherd puppy from a friend's litter unannounced. It took a lot of convincing but I finally managed to persuade my parents that I too would walk and feed and clean up after a brand new cuddly little puppy.

I'd named him Scampy after a cartoon character I faithfully followed in the New York Daily News. My father allowed me to keep the little pup provided I tie him up at the end of a long hallway just outside our third floor flat. And I did walk him and take care of him as I vowed I would.

We'd become quite a team Scamp and I. I reveled at the envious looks on my dogless friends' faces when I brought him to school for "show and tell." I'll never forget how everyone wanted to pet my little puppy and walk beside me in the schoolyard that day.

That warm-fuzzy feeling was abruptly short-circuited when at eight months old, Scampy began to chew on the linoleum carpet in the back of the hall. By the time it had been half torn apart, my father decided the dog was becoming too much of a nuisance. Summoning me one night to the dining room table, where all important household decisions were made, he told me that we could no longer keep Scampy.

No amount of crying or begging would change his mind. I carried on so until I was sent out into the hallway to spend the night with the innocent little pup who licked the salty tears from my eyes. I swore then and there that no matter what, I would never let anyone separate us.

But that was not to be. The next day my father told me that an acquaintance of his, actually a drinking buddy from Charlie's Bar and Grill, offered to "take the dog off our hands."

Slobbering hysterically and hiccuping with every breath, I gathered together Scampy's dish and toys and handed them over to my father who by this time had become in my mind a villain more evil than Captain Hook.

I soon discovered where he took Scampy and quickly set out to visit him. Climbing the stoop of a shingled six-family walk-up, I stretched up to ring the doorbell of the dog's new owner, but no one answered. Instead, I heard high-pitched howling yelps coming from the cellar door. Running down the steps I pressed my face close to the frosted glass basement window and cried "Scampy! Scampy!" but couldn't see inside.

I ran back and forth from the basement window to the bell, ringing and tapping to no avail. After about a half-hour I gave up and went home. But day after day, right after school, I went back to that basement window. At the very least I thought, Scampy knew that I had not completely abandoned him.

A week had passed when on one of my visits I noticed that the barking had stopped. I ran home and waited for my father to come home from work. "Scampy's not there," I cried, "what has that awful man done to my dog?"

"He barked too much," my father said. "The neighbors complained, so my buddy gave Scampy to someone who lives in the country. "The dog is where he belongs now, out in the open where he can run around and play," said my father, declaring the case closed.

I blamed him for my misery and the misery that he had caused Scampy. As I sat once again on the third-floor landing I secretly pledged to myself that someday, somehow, I would right the wrong that was inflicted upon me and my poor little friend at the tenderest stages of our lives.

But my children and husband knew nothing of Scamp or the circumstances surrounding my wanting a dog. After 30 years, I felt the time had come at last to make good on my pledge. My children were growing up quickly and before it was too late, I wanted them to know what it was like to have and love a puppy of their own.

A miniature Cockerspaniel, buff in color, was what my youngest and I chose at a kennel filled with newborn pups. We named her LuLu, after Ed Norton's childhood puppy, and brought her home to the rest of the family who'd expected their nice, neat little world to crumble that very day.

Luckily, it didn't happen that way. With time, LuLu charmed each member of the family, winning them over one by one. My eldest "aw don't get a dog," daughter crouches on all fours to play doggy-catch with LuLu on the living room floor every night. My son, whose macho attitude precludes being much of a snuggler, nuzzles his nose in LuLu's ear as he carries her, babylike, throughout the house. The youngest, who promised to "walk and feed and clean-up after a dog," has backed out of her original agreement, but still continues to allow LuLu into her bed at night.

As for my husband, he finally has someone to eagerly greet him when he walks in the door after a hard day's work.

Ironically, now they all fight over whom the dog likes best. An exercise in futility. Though she's stripped the lower edges of the kitchen wallpaper, tinkled on my fine imported rugs and wrecked havoc with trails of bubble gum, LuLu knows that she is loved by someone who will never, ever, even think of giving her away to some stranger... there was never a doubt in my mind that she loves me best.

JUST BETWEEN US

"What makes you cry so much? She's in paradise now," my mother-in-law tried to comfort me when my sister died.

I picked up a bottle of cologne and was about to spray it on as I customarily do during my morning ritual, when suddenly I realized I was going to visit my sister. Stopping in midair I put the bottle down. Rosemarie hated the smell of perfume, she always scrunched up her nose and pulled away from me whenever she got a waft of my usual sweet scent. Though she wouldn't be admonishing me now, since I'd be visiting her in the cemetery, the thought of doing something that might offend her, still keeps me connected.

Nine years older than me and born during the lean years of World War II, my sister always considered me, a product of the post-war baby boom, privileged and spoiled. I guess, in a sense, I was. She was a secretary who became a homemaker while I went to college and became a teacher. She married an automobile mechanic and I marred a business executive. She had a second home in the hardscrabble Catstkills, mine was in the trendy Hamptons. The only advantage it appeared she had over me was her blondness and thinness, compared to my dark olive skin and round figure.

If there was one single point of common ground between us though, it was our intense fear of dying.

The prospect of death haunted us ever since our mother died of colon cancer when she was fifty-five. We were always afraid that the same unpredictable scourge would suddenly surface and rob us of the rest of our lives too. There was a special meaning then, behind the call I made to my sister on the day she turned fifty-five and mockingly congratulated her for having made it to that magic number. She laughed with what I could hear was relief in her voice, the bad omen finally exorcized from our seemingly overactive imaginations.

What we didn't realize was it wasn't reaching fifty-five, but passing beyond it that would be the true test of our destinies. Two months after that fateful birthday my sister was diagnosed with pancreatic cancer. Six months later she died. Now, the fear that was once shared between us is a singular burden that has become almost too heavy to bear, especially since I subsequently developed breast cancer at age fifty and somehow survived the dreaded curse.

Standing on top of Rosemarie's grave, I feel it could be me buried under six feet of black earth and she looking down at my remains. One thing we were particularly attuned to were each others' fears. She surely would have been terrified of the bug and spider that scrambled out of the earth when I dug into it with a spade, the yellow jacket buzzing around her headstone would have upset her even more. If she were alive, she would have flailed and run away from it as she always did with flying insects. How incredibly bizarre that she's actually safe from that kind of danger now. Yet knowing what I know, I remain afraid for her.

She was claustrophobic too, and avoided having to take elevators or drive through tunnels. If she knew that she was sealed inside a steel box and placed deep under the ground, she'd thrash and pound and struggle to be free. Like me, the privileged sister. I'm the free one but only in a physical sense. Emotionally I'm trapped by words and melodies or smells that ricochet through my daily life and evoke my sister's memory, reminding me when I least expect it, that she is no longer a part of my world.

I go to the cemetery to reaffirm her existence. It's a place we used to meet to lay flowers at our mother's grave. On those days I always teased my sister for carting along an extra pair of old shoes to change into so she wouldn't muddy her car. She would never have believed it, but now I change into an old pair of shoes too. Just like not wearing perfume, it's my own peculiar way of hanging onto shreds of my sister's memory.

With the more recent death of my father, who died of cardiac arrest five months after Rosemarie passed away, the cemetery is all the more compelling as a repository for the nuclear family around which I still hover. When I first went to visit all three of my family members there, I asked my husband to join me to provide moral support. What I didn't expect, was for him to stop at the cemetery's business office to inquire about available plots.

I protested his inquiry as cold and insensitive, but the idea of purchasing my own grave became more appealing as I realized I could actually manage to control some part of my death. Unlike my sister, I wanted the experience of knowing the place where I would spend eternity. It was eerily satisfying to purchase two side-by-side crypts on the very top row of an indoor mausoleum, chosen primarily because I don't like anything on top of me and my husband can't stand crawly things.

Cemetery visits now follow a ritualistic pattern in which I am part of the loop. I first stop at my parents' graves where my father's heart and soul and being are fresh in my mind. I mourn with even more sorrow the loss of my mother's memory, which has become but a shadow of a long forgotten past. Next, I am drawn to my own eternal resting place. It pleases me to see that even on a gloomy day, light reflects steadily off the arched ceiling and glistening facade.

Facing my own inevitable death gives me the courage to make a final stop at my sister's grave. Witnessing her greatest fear come true has traumatized me into savoring my own life every day as I live it. If that makes me privileged, I have learned life's greatest lesson from one who didn't consider herself so.

BAD VIBES

My mother-in-law often showed me the scar from a benign lump removed from her breast to illustrate the number of operations she'd suffered through. At the time, I treated it very much like the litany of other stories she told and retold time and again.

"You look soooo good," is a remark usually meant and taken as a compliment, unless of course, you've had cancer, then it becomes a reminder that others expect you to kick the bucket sometime soon. My body goes tense, like a cat in danger, every time well-meaning acquaintances tell me how wonderful I look, because I feel I'm being ever so subtly scrutinized for telltale signs of my impending death.

It was during a routine annual check-up when I was 49 my internist felt a lump in my right breast. I jumped when she palpated it. That was a good sign, she said, probably only a cyst or swollen gland. "Keep an eye on it for two weeks and call me if there's no change," was her advice.

By coincidence, a week later, while accompanying my youngest daughter on a visit to a breast surgeon for a fibroadenoma, a benign lump she had to have removed, the thought suddenly popped into my head to have the doctor examine me too. Echoing my internist, the breast surgeon told me not to worry: it could simply be a clogged milk duct. But a chill slid up my spine when I saw the doctor's confident smile turn to a frown as she probed my right breast for a fine needle biopsy.

When she, and not her office assistants, called me three days later, intuitively I knew the news wouldn't be good.

"Is it positive?" I asked, making the first move. "Yes," she countered, checkmating me. "Go straight to the hospital, I've arranged for you to have a mammogram there, then meet me right afterwards at my office," she instructed in a detached authoritarian manner.

I hung up and shakily started dialing my husband's work number, realizing only after it rang a number of times, he was already in the air on a flight to London. It would be six more hours before I could reach him: until then, I was on my own. Thoughts of my mother and sister dying of cancer and my father's suffering from it, blinked through my mind like a slide show. Okay, I thought, what makes me so special? Now it's my turn.

That logic didn't transfer from my brain to my jittery hands. They shook so, I had a hard time inserting the key into the car's ignition. It took an enormous amount of control to keep my foot on the brake as I approached red lights, I couldn't wait, had to stay in motion, keep the car in sync with my trembling body and racing mind. Turn, stop, left, right, park, walk, enter, register, wait.

I managed to hold myself together until the receptionist called my name. Haltingly, as if in slow motion, I rose and burst like a bubble into frightened tears. A kindly nurse nestled me into the crook of her arm and led me away from dozens of pairs of inquiring eyes, off to an examining room, where I sat, staring down at the balled up wads of wet tissues that materialized in my hands

Someone knocked. A breast-cancer survivor who worked at the hospital was summoned to comfort me. But her upbeat, complacence at having had and beat cancer, was no consolation. I was still hanging onto the hope that a mammogram would show this was all a mistake. Soon enough, I learned it wasn't. Numbly, I went through the motions of having my breasts squeezed into flat pancakes, and waited in a timeless daze for the results. Three doctors walked in holding clipboards. The leader of the pack took my hand and brought me quickly back to reality—the tumor was larger than expected, 2 centimeters, already at stage II. Abruptly, I pulled away, angry at her and doctors in general, all of them.

Hadn't it been drummed into our heads ad-infinitum, mammograms are supposed to detect cancer before it can be felt? I'd had mammograms for five straight years at that very hospital—the last one, just ten months before—why wasn't it discovered then? I was angrier still, that only a month earlier, this lump was not discovered during a manual breast exam on a regular visit to my gynecologist—a lump that was already 2 centimeters—stage II not I—was not felt by someone who was supposed to be an expert at this sort of thing. I followed all the rules, took all the precautions for early detection seriously, checked myself methodically, and still it somehow slipped by me. My head spun.

"How could it have grown so fast in such a short time?" I raged, from the other side of the breast surgeon's desk. She slowly shook her head from side to side in a non-answer. She didn't know either. Checking her schedule, she found an opening at the clinic in two days time, "let's take the lump out to see what we're dealing with," she said, tipping back in her chair." I felt fortunate to fill the slot and made the quick decision on the spot, by myself, to have it done quickly.

Upon hearing my angry and, by then, hysterical account of the traumatic developments that occurred while he was in flight, my husband turned abruptly around and flew right back home. With no time to waste, he immediately began to call specialists and scout out contacts at various hospitals while I scoured through breast cancer books, each of us trying to convince the other with details we'd gleaned, that my case wasn't so bad.

I trusted the surgeon who'd be doing the procedure, since she'd operated successfully on lumps in both my daughters' breasts, but as I lay on the gurney awaiting my own lumpectomy, I asked why she wouldn't be removing the lymph nodes under my armpit at the same time, since I'd read that lymph node involvement is a clear sign of cancer's spread. She stood back puzzled, said we'd agreed to do it this way. In a moment of clarity before the anesthesia was injected into my veins, I lost confidence in the person who hadn't really explained all the options available to me, the person who was about to slice into my breast with a knife.

As it is, when I woke up, I learned the lump measured 2.4 centimeters. How fast was this thing growing? Lab results revealed, pretty fast, the grade of the tumor was rated nine. From what I'd read, the scale from low grade to high grade tumors ranged from one to four—mine was nine!

"What does that mean?" I asked the surgeon incredulously.

Again she shook her head in an uncomfortable non-answer, then went on to explain how there were still "dirty margins," which meant she hadn't gotten it all. Besides, there was evidence of necrosis—a sign the cells were dying off because they were multiplying at such a fast rate they'd outgrown their blood supply.

If I needed another operation, I decided this surgeon wouldn't be the one to do it. Instead, I did what most women do in this situation, consulted with many different doctors. I had two options: another lumpectomy with a wider incision, leaving me with half a breast, or a mastectomy, leaving me without a breast—both involved removing the lymph nodes and a hospital stay. In my case, I didn't think having half a breast would be better than no breast at all. What really convinced me to go with the more extensive procedure was a conversation I'd had with an anesthesiologist.

"What happens to the breast after it's removed in a mastectomy?" I asked.

He told me the entire tissue sample is analyzed for cancer.

That convinced me to go with the mastectomy. I felt safer knowing my entire breast would be looked at under a microscope, especially since I didn't trust the rapid development of the cancer growing inside of me and what the doctors couldn't tell me about it. My husband agreed.

As I lay on the operating table a second time, my new surgeon asked if I was sure I wanted the whole breast removed. His skittishness was understandable, since he was operating in the blind — having to lop off my breast without knowing whether or not the cancer had spread to my lymph nodes. But this time around, I sensed that I needed to take control over my own destiny.

"Off with the breast!" I commanded.

The good news was there was no sign of cancer in any of the 27 lymph nodes removed, which could have been bad news since I might not have needed the mastectomy after all, except that another kind of cancer called Paget's disease was growing on the nipple of that very breast, so it was actually good the entire breast had come off.

My first reaction was relief. Then my blood percolated with anger as I thought no doctor had taken me seriously three years before when I'd gone to them with a flaky scab on the nipple of my right breast.

"Could this scaliness be a sign of Paget's disease?" I asked my gynecologist after reading about the nipple-related cancer condition in Dr. Susan Love's Breast Book.

"Oh, no," she said, "this looks to me like a spider bite."

I was taken aback. Try as I might, I couldn't fathom how a spider could bite my breast without my feeling the pinch. Just the thought of it was creepy.

"My gynecologist said this is a spider bite, but I'm worried it's Paget's disease," I told a well-known breast surgeon at a major New York hospital.

"There's no discharge or puckering, it looks like a skin ailment to me," she said, and advised me to see a dermatologist.

"I thought this was Paget's disease, but a top breast surgeon told me it was a skin condition," I told the third doctor. He promptly prescribed a cortisone cream which I conscientiously slathered onto my breast after I brushed my teeth, for three son-of-a-bitching years! I was learning now, I didn't have to.

"I diagnosed myself with Paget's Disease three years ago," I said bitterly to the breast surgeon who delivered the news about this unexpected finding.

"Why didn't you bring it to my attention?" he asked, as if I were remiss.

I was struck dumb.

"Because three idiots who call themselves doctors first told me a spider bit me, then they said I had a skin condition." His face colored.

"I'm no doctor, but don't you think at least one of the Three Stooges who examined me should have taken a biopsy of my nipple?"

"That's a good question," was all he could offer.

Extending his hands out to my shoulders, he looked at me straight on and said he was glad I'd insisted on having the mastectomy because the Paget's Disease would have necessitated another surgery in the future.

So there I was, left to ruminate with my happy, sorry self.

This tragi-comedy of errors taught me to trust my instincts about my own body over any doctors, and not to trust cancer under any circumstances. It's sneaky.

I'm reminded of that whenever someone catches me off-guard and tells me how good I look.

BRED, SEPALEE & PITZA

Take 7 lbs. of floure
Make a hole and put 3 small potatoes
And a handful of salt in it.
Mix 5 cups of water in senter.
Add about a block of yest
In a little warm water.
Keep adding more floure.
Mix, punch, turn over, punch
Punch, punch, punch, punch.

(Recipe of a 6-year-old grand-daughter)

Every time my Italian-speaking mother-in-law came knocking at my front door when I was first married, I was in dread of what she would bring.

Sometimes it was homemade soap, my mother-in-law made from excess lard she'd carved off two-weeks worth of meat which she insisted I use to wash my dishes and clothes. Another time it would be bitter-tasting chickory leaves she'd picked on the grounds of a nearby park, which I was then expected to boil and drink the liquid from, before her very eyes.

But what I feared most, was seeing her lug a ten-pound bag of flour up my front steps in her shopping cart, for I knew the next 18 hours would be devoted solely to turning it into bread. My house became a war zone, she was the general, and I, being the only other female in her family of two sons, was conscripted into her one-person army. It boiled down to her giving orders and my taking them, something I was not used to doing even with my new husband.

What I was up against was a woman who never wore store-bought clothes.

"Beatrice [Be-ah-tree-chay], ho bisogno di una pentola grande (I need a big pot), un coltello che taglia (a sharp knife), un bicchiere di acqua tiepida (a glass of warm water). And so it went as I was ordered about, following her commands like a dutiful daughter-in-law, but inevitably the pot would always be too small, the knife too dull or the water too cool and my mother-in law would turn to me in exasperation. I could tell she was thinking I'd never make a good Italian wife for her son.

There were not only cultural and language barriers that stood between us, I was, after all, Italian-American and so were my parents, but there were generational differences as well. How could I possibly understand the significance of a bread-baking ritual that carried this very poor and independent woman through The Depression and two World Wars in a land and time that were foreign to me? That because her husband had emigrated to America 24 years before she did, she was solely responsible for providing for what was then her only child? That she found a way of doing so by hiding sacks of rationed flour under her dress, pretending to be pregnant in order to bypass the authorities?

She knew instinctively what was needed to prepare what was surely for her, the staff of life, and any newfangled pots and pans or especially ideas of my own, could not be allowed to jeopardize her timeworn process of proven success. Taking a 2-inch chunk of yeast she'd picked up at the local Italian bakery for free the day before, she'd dissolve it in about five cups of warm water (trying to establish exact measurements with my mother-in-law was an absurdity). Taking a generous handful of flour, "la generalissima" would throw it down onto my kitchen tabletop, with a fine layer settling on the floor, chairs and overhead light fixture. Emptying about seven pounds of flour into a huge half-moon bowl, she opened a crater-sized well in the center in which she placed three small "patate sane" (mashed potatoes) and a handful of salt. Gradually she'd work the yeast mixture into the flour, slowly, rhythmically, in a counterclockwise motion.

When all of the liquid was blended into the flour, my mother-in-law would lay the formidable mass before her, as if it were a newborn baby. She'd take the furthest end of the dough, fold it toward her and push it back with the heel of her hand, then jab at it repeatedly with her fists. This was when I was actually allowed to touch the dough, helping to fold, turn, push and punch. But that didn't last long. She'd watch, eagle-eyed, and when my arms would tire and the pace would slow, she would knock me aside with her hip, and continue to knead the dough until every last scrap was absorbed into its elasticity.

A sweet-sour fragrance permeated the kitchen as a large cotton towel was draped over the birthing bread. The biggest pot in my house was called into service as an incubator. My mother-in-law coated the inside of it with olive oil before placing the dough inside, and covered it with a lid. This is the point at which the real bonding between the dough and its maker took place, for my mother-in-law attached herself to that pot as if her life depended on it.

She even took the pot to bed with her. Placing it on the floor, not two feet from her pillow, she monitored the dough's progress, punching it down to let air bubbles out every couple of hours throughout the night. Once, when she insisted the living room couch would be more comfortable to sleep on, I had a hard time convincing her that my dog might smell the pot near the couch, knock it over, eat the rising dough, and explode! It took fifteen minutes to persuade her to place the pot on top of a coffee table. She was not happy, and let me know in no uncertain terms that she was making a supreme sacrifice.

At daybreak, my mother-in-law would be up and already aproned. Before I could get past her to make coffee, I was once again pulled into the fray. By this time, the dough had risen to the point of lifting the pot's lid. Turning it out onto the table with a practiced hand, my mother-in-law sliced it into four sections, two to be used for making bread and the other two for pizza and zeppole.

The bread loaves were set atop heavy black pans that had been sprinkled with flour. When they were finally ready for baking, there was always a big fuss made about the temperature of my electric oven. It never quite matched the quality of brick, coal and finally gas-fired ovens my mother-in-law had been used to, but I'm convinced she raised this issue to absolve herself from blame should the bread turn out poorly once it left her hands.

It never did. The huge golden loaves were always crusty on the outside, airy and chewy inside — the kind of bread that was not meant for buttering, but for heartier purposes, like dipping into the natural juices of fresh cooked roasts, for shoveling peppers and wiping up leftover pasta sauce.

When she was finally able to part with them, my mother-in-law would clutch each loaf of bread to her breast and carve into it with the knife moving toward her. She'd groan as each slice fell to the table, and I was never quite sure whether those groans were part of the final stage of delivery or if she'd accidentally sliced through to her heart.

Barely an hour would pass before the black pans were wiped down and lightly oiled for pizza. My mother-in-law stretched hand-sized slices of dough into rectangles and rubbed olive oil over each one. Using a large black knife, she'd cut chunks of fresh, drippy plum tomatoes, skin, seeds and all, and let them fall onto the dough in haphazard fashion. Minced parsely, garlic and freshly grated Parmesan cheese were strewn about on top (it dawned on me that red, white and green were the national colors of Italy for a reason)!

With only one section of dough left I knew things would finally be winding down. That portion was cut into small 2x2-inch squares, which my mother-in-law deftly dropped into a tiny pot of hot vegetable oil. I tried, but repeatedly lost, the argument that a larger pot would take less time, but was told that was wasteful. When the zeppole were cool enough to handle, I was always tempted to sprinkle powdered sugar on them as they do at Italian feasts, but my mother-in-law took offense. She felt that her zeppole didn't need anything to enhance their flavor.

The whole process from start to finish lasted eighteen hours, and at least two days more for me to clean up and regain my physical and mental strength.

I never would have believed that what I once dreaded, I now miss with an ache. When she reached her nineties, my mother-in-law no longer had the stamina to mix and turn and punch ten pounds of unwieldly dough into submission. Longing for the delicious old-world bread and pizza and zeppole my husband and children looked to me, the natural heir-apparent, to make it for them. The thought was overwhelming.

I've come to realize that what we experienced was a work of art, born by necessity and inspired by a labor of love. No matter how I put the ingredients together, the underlying elements would always be missing.

MOTHER WRITER

When I first started writing a column for my hometown newspaper in 1984, my mother-in-law intimated I should be home cooking, cleaning and taking care of my family. She knew no other way, but I'd already experienced a taste of higher learning and the working world.

Living in a suburban village on Long Island in the 1980's, I participated in all the parent-driven activities when my children were small, but, while my three little fledglings were exposed to new experiences every day, my learning curve was at a standstill. Mike's job started to take him to faraway places then, sometimes for twenty days at a time, and I needed to fill the emptiness.

I joined a book club but it met only once a month.

What eventually peaked my interest was a writing workshop at the local library of a nearby village. Its genre was short stories. I joined when my youngest was in nursery school, she and my other two children watched with suspicious anxiety as their mother slipped into a gear they were unfamiliar with. It was "mommy's mission" to buy a typewriter and set up a desk, find a corner of space in the house where she could focus on writing and pursue her own goals.

Propelling me forward was a long-held desire to write; ever since I listed journalism as my prospective major in college and learned it wasn't offered, I carried the torch of that unrealized ambition.

Though I soon discovered short-stories weren't my strong point, what seemed to flow naturally was the way words tumbled out onto the typewritten page.

Encouraged by my fellow workshop writers, I sent a short essay I'd written about the sights and smells of walking through the aisles of the local five-and-dime store to my hometown newspaper and it was accepted. The pay was a mere five dollars—but it didn't matter because my husband and children looked at me through new eyes after that.

However meager that payment was, I worked hard on that story, and others to follow, and when neighbors and townspeople began to recognize my byline I felt my identity morph from ho-hum mother to valued professional.

The transformation was not without pitfalls.

A book-length history project I took on for the town's tricentennial turned into a public cat-fight when one of the dowager's of the town's "old guard" used my research to write a story under her own byline. I was incensed and further inflamed when another old biddy said in a condescending honey-dipped voice that I was still wet behind the ears and suggested I read Proust.

I acted insulted but cried behind closed doors.

My children, meanwhile, had to deal with the side-effects of mommy's testiness when they took rulers or notepads from my desk, or cut into the middle of my phone conversations to ask where the freshly bought donuts were. All three of them were offended when I taped a sign on my office door that warned, "Do Not Enter," but I learned the hard way I had to maintain some sort of professionalism when, one day while interviewing the county executive, my adolescent son forgot his keys and, alternately rang the bell and threw pebbles at my office window which started the dog barking. The scene was a cacophonus three-ring circus.

Sometimes, I took my role as reporter a bit too far, as my husband is apt to claim. He was horrified when during 1985's Hurricane Gloria, a huge willow tree toppled in our backyard and I used that as an excuse for us to seek shelter at the local high school. He was worried about our safety—fearing another tree could fall on our car as we drove through a raging storm, while I was hot on the trail of a developing story. At the high school's command central, I interviewed county officials about evacuation plans and pieced together the accounts of storekeepers and homeowners who abandoned their wind-swept buildings. My by-lined story ran in two parts on page one and three. My husband still maintains leaving the house in the middle of a category 4 hurricane was the stupidest thing he's ever done.

That headlined story eventually propelled me to delve deeper into reporting with an investigative slant, but my editor—a 22 year-old just out of J-school grad—pulled the plug on that. Our publisher, he said, wasn't looking for sensational pieces that caused a stir, but wanted "happy news." In killing a story about a sketchy real-estate deal, the young know-it-all added salt to my wounded ego by calling my writing "lackluster."

To prove him wrong, I pelted the editor of the regional section of The New York Times with article ideas until he gave me assignments just to get me off his back.

As if spontaneously sprung from a dormant shell, my first few Times' stories broke-forth in great sweeping strides across all four columns of the front page—they were about government budgets, the shortage of Catholic priests, land acquisition and political in-fighting—I hit my stride and was on a roll—sans Proust and with hardly a lack of luster.

I was surprised at how easily I gained access to and interviewed government officials, CEO's and entertainers, when, in fact, my very own relatives continued to intimidate me. My father and mother-in-law as well as most of the rest of my family didn't read The Times, and they had no clue about my life outside their own predictable domains.

My sister, though, who heard from others about my various stories, vicariously enjoyed my notoriety and giddily asked to accompany me one day when I left a houseful of guests to check on a "tip" that an illegal event was to take place at the county museum. When we arrived, she backed off, suddenly turned chicken, and refused to go inside with me.

She tried again to become involved in my new career by pitching a story idea to me about the popularity of the western dance classes she was taking. After I interviewed the people she put me in touch with and wrote the story she was pissed that I hadn't included a quote from her.

"You're such a goody-two-shoes," she said, adding that our last names were different so no one would have made the connection. "Why couldn't you give me the thrill of seeing my name in The New York Times?"

I rose above the fray, telling her journalists just didn't put their relatives in stories, but when she unexpectedly died a year later, I was haunted by the guilt of not having granted her that one last pleasure.

Perhaps I was too uptight after all. Maybe I should have read Proust and worked on my lackluster writing. You can never really tell which battles were worth fighting for until they are over.

GASTRONOMIC MANIA

To stay in her good graces, one had to bring a "buon appetito" (good appetite) to my mother-in-law's table. Fortunately, that happened to be one of her Sicilian daughter-in-law's best traits.

There I was, sitting in a diner innocently biting into my triple-decker turkey sandwich when I caught the twinkling eye of an elderly woman passing by on her way to the ladies' room. She made it a point to stop directly in front of me, smile broadly and say "good appetite."

I stopped chewing and remained, cheeks stuffed like a chipmunk.

"Did she say good appetizer?" my daughter asked. I shook my head, swallowed what was in my mouth, and repeated exactly the old crone's words.

"What nerve!" she exclaimed, expecting me to be mortified too. But I knew, in a split second of intuitive communication, this perfect stranger caught me unabashedly involved in an activity I normally try to hide from the rest of the world — savoring food.

Though I'm sure the blunt remark was well-meant, the old lady probably thought she was paying me a compliment, but what really offended me was being "outted" over a dry, stick-in-your-throat turkey sandwich, with a measly slice of tomato and limp scrap of lettuce, no mayo, no bacon — it wasn't even my lunch, but dinner! I can only imagine what the doting, do-gooder would have said had she seen me enjoying my dream meal — a juicy burger smeared with onions, a mountain of crinkle-cut French-fries with gobs of ketchup and a thick, creamy vanilla shake!

I wish I could eat to live rather than live to eat, but a long line of Cicio girls just weren't built that way. The majority of us are big girls, bottom heavy with thick thighs and pumpkin-sized bums. "Roley-poley," my dad used to call me — completely unaware that my unbudgeable size-fourteen was solely the result of his hefty-mother's genes.

Most of the time, my passion for food emerges when I'm alone. Not that I'm a closet-eater like a nervous squirrel coveting a stash of buried nuts, but more of a well-tempered cow relishing cud in a faraway pasture, mooing my palatable approval to no one in particular.

Since I wasn't breast fed, it could be I've been searching for a succulent breast all my life. A single sandwich is never satisfying enough; I always need another half to quell my watering tongue. And while a slice of pie is my limit in front of company, long after they're gone, the remaining wedges cry out "eat me, eat me" from the fridge until I surrender.

As easily as I can recite the multiplication tables and Shakespeare's soliloquies stored somewhere in the furthest corners of my brain, so too can my taste-buds recall the unforgettable meals that have passed through my alimentary canal.

France was the first place to wet my as-yet unschooled appetite for fine foods. I'd just turned thirty-one and was five months pregnant with my third child and it was goose liver of all things, that started my salivary juices flowing. My husband cajoled me into taking just one bite of this mud-colored delicacy on my first transatlantic flight abroad, and I ordered it as an appetizer for every meal that followed inside the Rues and Quai's of Paris and outside its arrondissemonts. Soon enough, I was lured and hooked by the delectable duo of caviar and champagne during cocktail hour, the perfumy seduction of white truffles shaved over each entree, brie and chevre slathered like butter on stiff crackers at a separate course altogether, and sinfully decadent souffles for dessert.

The extent of my gastronomic breakthrough became apparent to my husband when I merely gasped, yet continued to consume, the "canard" I was served at the famed Moulin de Mougins in south of France, after master chef Roger Verge revealed he used duck's blood to make the dark, heady sauce. "Quel damage!"

Until then, the only foreign food I'd eaten was in Mexico on my honeymoon, and the experience was far from gustatory. Lured to a tantalizing seafood buffet spread out before a romantic Acapulco lagoon, I quickly fell victim to something called "Montezuma's Revenge" and landed in the hospital with intravenous bottles attached to my arms.

Ah, but French food, from sole meuniere at a bistro along the Champs Elysee to charcroute at the haute Cafe Lipp, persuaded my wary tongue to dip into the cuisines of varied other cultures.

And I did so with increasing enthusiasm. In the Middle East, I scooped hummus at its place of origin, drank mint tea offered by rug merchants in underground souks and learned that pistachios weren't red. That really amazed me, as did the tenderness of whole baked fish encrusted with salt derived from mineral deposits that sat in huge mounds off the coasts of Dubai and Abu-Dhabi. On rare visits to private homes in these exotic places, every room, even the bathrooms, were infused with the fragrance of basmati rice which I discovered was stored in large quantities, like American potatoes, in 5 lb. bags.

Couscous served that same purpose in Morocco. I sampled that tiny, delicate grain in Casablanca and Marakeesh, mixed with cumin-flavored shanks of lamb in large earthen pots, scooping it as I did the hummus, but with pizza-sized rounds of unleavened bread instead of pita. That part of the world tends to scoop a lot. My husband recounts how he's spent many a business dinner seated on his haunches before a whole spit-roasted goat, pulling it apart and consuming it, along with rice, using only his hands.

Further north, in a different oil-producing country, the Italian land of my ancestors, I became acquainted with golden crude. The first press of olives during the harvest season yields the most valued oil of the meaty fruit and is typically used to enhance flavor; supposedly, it's too precious to use for cooking. I humbly drizzled this light, virginal liquid over a mushroom so large, it filled my entire plate at a restaurant in the Jewish ghetto of Rome, where we dined al fresco. I mistakenly thought the waiter brought me a steak.

"No, No, Signora — this is a portobello mushroom. When it's in season we serve it as a main dish," he said.

"Ah, paradiso!"

Again I mistook for something else the large round circles of meat my relatives in Sicily were sauteeing atop a blisteringly hot stove in their cramped farmhouse kitchen. I told them I'd never seen such big veal cutlets in the States, and they laughed.

"Oh no, cara cugina, this is not veal, it's goat meat." It was chewy, but I managed to wash it down with husky red wine that was readily replenished into carafes from large stainless steel containers that were stored behind doors and used for consumption on a daily basis like basmati rice in the Middle East.

Whatever else can be said of Italy, you simply can't get a bad meal in any of its restaurants. Even the worst pizzas and pastas are at the very least, palatable.

The same can't be said of England where bangers and mash, meat pies and Yorkshire Puddings are so dense, they pass through the intestines like thick cement. I learned this the hard way at a lunch hosted by an old acquaintance at Claridge's. Wrongly, I assumed "mixed grill" would be an assortment of tasty ribs and chops when I ordered it from the hotel's fancy menu. To my horror, what arrived was a dark jumble of organ meats — gnarly kidneys and hearts — whatever little of which passed through my lips caused me to wretch.

On the receiving end of this experience, my husband suggested the next time I meet old friends, I do so for tea. I did and was forever smitten with the tradition. Indulging in gentle dollops of clotted cream on warm-baked scones and crescent sandwiches filled with minced cucumbers and chives turned out to be a less risky culinary adventure. And never would I have dreamed there were so many varieties of tea — all brewed with loose leaves in ceramic teapots covered with cozies, and poured through strainers into delicate china cups.

I thought I'd have the same happy experience with Japanese tea but its algae-like pond water appearance prompted the same gagging response as the organ meats. I naively ordered it from room service upon my arrival in Tokyo thinking it would be a palliative for the bad experience I'd had with creamed crabmeat served aboard the plane. But the slimy green concoction was not the antidote I'd hoped for. What finally helped, was sticky rice.

I ate it exclusively for the next twenty-four hours and upon feeling better, began to flap my chopsticks into sushi and shabu-shabu as if I were Madama Butterfly. I sampled all kinds of exotica, from hundred year old quail eggs to soybean sweetcakes, but said "So sorry," to broth garnished with floating fish heads and the evil "fugu," — poisonous fish livers the Japanese pay 500,000 yen, or 500 dollars for, to experience the titillating thrill of momentarily having the back of their tongues paralyzed.

New Orleans is the one place stateside I've found to be as exciting culinary-wise. Were I to be offered my last meal on death row, I'd request the two-inch high, sugar-dusted beignets customarily served for breakfast along the Mississippi riverboat wharves. Those fluffy delights and fist-sized crawfish encased in their own bugeyed-shells cooked Cajun-style, I've never seen duplicated anywhere else. I don't know whether alligator or catfish that are widely featured on menus in the French Quarter are as tasty because I wasn't able, psychologically, to get past their mudflat lifestyle.

Elsewhere in the States, that little old lady from the diner would never have caught me enjoying the still-half-frozen surf n' turf with brick-hard stuffed potatoes served in one of Muncie, Indiana's leading restaurants. Her eyes wouldn't have twinkled watching me dig into the blob of red tomato sauce splayed sloppily straight from the can, over a dish of pasty-white spaghetti in Burlington, Vermont. Nor would she have bothered to even stop if she saw the look of utter revulsion on my face after swallowing fried eggs cooked on a greasy grill at a truck-stop on the Arizona side of the Grand Canyon.

There's no way she would have known this, or anything else about my personal gastronomic history based on one little chomp on a dry turkey sandwich.

CATASTROPHE

Donna Maria had a cat to kill the mice that nibbled away at her flour sacks when she lived in Italy, but there was absolutely no way was I ever going to have one in my house. That's what I told my youngest daughter the very first day she made the rash decision to buy a blue Abyssinian kitten and take care of it in her own apartment.

"This is not about you, Ma," she snipped.

"Okay," I said, taken aback. I desperately wanted to believe that, but was wary of her coping skills given the turmoil she'd been through over the previous two years. A life-shattering nervous breakdown pretty much stripped my youngest child of any semblance of control over her behavior, and buying a cat, I felt, was yet another far-reaching attempt to assume responsibility that she wasn't quite up to handling.

I'd already felt beaten down from fits and starts of impulsive behavior that left me holding the bag for a health club membership she let flounder, overdue bills, and failed efforts to complete college courses and craft workshops she'd enrolled in. Still, empathizing with her shaky plight, I tried with each successive regression to understand the enormous task she faced of putting her shattered life back together, piece by broken piece.

To maintain my own sanity amid the chaos and confusion, I had to draw a line as to what I would tolerate, and the cat was on the other side of it. I never liked cats. The sneaky way they slink around as if they're always on the prowl, and dart about like kites in the wind, unnerves me. I hate the way they unexpectedly jump up onto high places and imperiously observe the action below, looking down as if everything was beneath their dignity. I never liked their innate need to claw and rub, their finickiness with food and aloof social demeanor. Add to that my allergy to dander, for certain, cats were the least endearing household pets I cared to live with.

But sure as I called it, when a sudden setback resulted in my daughter having to move back to a treatment facility where no pets were allowed, what to do with her cat, became a major concern bordering on hysteria. A quickly devised plan to have a friend who lived near the facility watch the six month old kitty, with the proviso that my daughter would visit every day to feed and care for her, fell apart at the very last minute.

Pitying our painfully thin daughter's inability to cope, standing face-to-face with her doe-eyed and somber stare into oblivion, my husband told her not to worry, he would find a temporary home for the cat. Precipitously, I dissolved into the incredibly shrinking woman, torn between taking this monumental pressure off of my daughter's already tortured mind, and preserving my own.

Our 22-year-old merely hugged us goodbye, but cried big heaping sobs over leaving the cat: it meant that much to her.

"There is absolutely no way I'm going to keep a cat in my house," I told my husband as we sat in separate but equal sized bucket-seats on the two-and-a-half hour ride home. I knew I had to hold my ground, state my limits from the very start, otherwise I'd be swallowed up by his neediness too.

"No, no, this is just temporary," he promised, patting my crossed hands." Give me a week and I'll find someone to take the cat." I sighed, wanting to believe that. Edgily I glanced at the backseat every few minutes to observe the caged-cat's reaction to the upheaval in her short life and wondered if she'd be as traumatized as my daughter was in hers.

Pulling up to my husband's office, he leaned over, pecked me on the cheek, slid out of the driver's side, grabbed his attache case and walked hurriedly through the revolving door. That left — just the two of us — me, and my arch-enemy who, though barely 1/300th my size, held all the power.

I expected Angelina to be like spit-fire, take no prisoners Tomb Raider Angelina Jolie, the actress she was named after. Her belongings were enough to give me lockjaw, what with a carrying cage, litter box, scratching post, balls, water and food dishes, tins of wet and bags of dry foods and the worst, litter itself. Beyond that, my greatest concern was how our 14-year-old cockerspaniel would react to a temporary boarder not of her own breeding. Lulu was extremely territorial with other dogs, marking her own spot with her own effluent whenever they invaded her domain. And of course, there was the female thing too — LuLu and Angelina — could two women, three with me, peacefully co-exist in the same milieu?

All of my family's eyes were focused on me. "It's not fair for you to have to take this responsibility," my two other children sympathized, at the same time pointing out their own sensitive allergic reactions to cats. "How's she doing?" my husband asked in increasingly annoying hourly phone calls.

I tried to remain calm by staying in control. At first I kept the sleek blue-gray and curly buff-colored critters isolated from each other. They sat on either side of a door that separated them, ears perked up with a mixture of excitement and fear. I worried about LuLu baring her teeth and snapping at the tiny newcomer and I worried about the newcomer's tearing at LuLu's eyes.

When I finally opened the door, curiosity got the cat, and dog, and what they actually did was sniff each other's noses and private parts. Slowly, Angelina began to explore the wide expanse of connecting hallways that linked bedrooms, a foyer that branched out into kitchen, and the dining and living rooms, reminding me of the awe with which first-time visitors take-in the vastness of Disney World. It occurred to me then, that Angelina had never had this much space to roam around in, and I found myself shadowing her to see her reaction to new discoveries.

LuLu followed her too, everywhere. Probably for different reasons than mine. I sensed LuLu was trying to gauge just how much of a threat this new presence in our household posed to her own, rather lofty status as the single most adored pet in the family. As it turned out, her instincts were just as right as mine when it came to the impact Angelina would have on our so-far, comfortably placid, lifestyles.

She most likely spied Angelina in action, whereas I saw only the results. All around I'd begun to notice telltale signs that Angelina had stuck her nose in a planter, hopped atop a table or into my tub. Leafy fronds on the floor and a tablecloth askew were benign signs Angelina had been there and done that. Even more telling were the culpable paw-prints on my dark wood furniture, that I purposely left to show my husband, and which we both giggled over.

It took only 48 hours for me to fall under this feline's enchanting spell. "We'll keep the cat for now," I told my husband who was thrilled not to have the responsibility anymore. He knew that I knew, he thought I'd be a soft touch all along.

But I still had the mixed duo to contend with.

On two occasions, LuLu came over to me trembling, a sign that something was terribly wrong. Heeding her urgency, I found yet further evidence of Angelina's adventurous escapades, a dish of muffins bitten into on the kitchen counter and a half-dozen long-tapered candles toppled like pick-up sticks on the cocktail table.

"Ah—hah! Caught you in the act! I'm telling mom! You're in big trouble now sister," I imagined LuLu saying when she came to me and shook.

She seemed miffed at my a half-hearted attempt to punish the cat, especially since much of Angelina's mischief-making took place in the living room, the one place I'd always held sacrosanct from desecration. The aging canine, almost 98 in dog years, probably sensed the laissez-faire treatment I was showering on this young upstart was very different from her own strict-upbringing. She didn't like it too, that the cat began to take advantage of her weak eyes and legs and heart.

Once Angelina became comfortable in her surroundings and coyly realized her youth gave her a head-start, she playfully teased the old lady by invading her private space. She'd gingerly slip into the kitchen and drink from LuLu's water dish, sit tauntingly in her fluffy dogbed, or catapult right over her while she was asleep, causing the poor old dog to jolt awake and take chase. It always ended in humiliation for the nonagenarian who couldn't keep up, and always found herself looking up at the impish pussy somewhere high out of reach. This was the ultimate insult for LuLu, for try as she might, she could no longer propel herself onto the couch or bed or a lap—and was now relegated to watching this spry little ball of fur do so, and capture our hearts in the process.

To my complete astonishment, Angelina was winning me over. I laughed as if I'd been tickled at the comical way she pranced around with a little blue ball dangling out of one side of her mouth like a cigar. And I wished I'd caught on videotape the vision of her standing on hind legs, staring into the clothes dryer, her head revolving with each tumble of the drum.

Not that her presence hasn't caused problems too. LuLu has eaten more than her share of flaked salmon and trout, because Angelina prefers to pick at her food throughout the day, so keeping the dog away from the cat's dish, as well as snooping and sniffing in her litter box requires constant vigilance. As for the little prima donna herself, she's learned to play hide and seek. I've lost her for hours at a time only to be bowled-over when she jumps out from under the sink, a clothes closet, the door to the laundry and even—merciful Lord—the elevator!!

She likes sequestering herself quietly in shopping bags, atop laundry baskets, under bedskirts and walks silently from chair to chair under the cloak of a draped table cloth in the dining room.

"Here kitty, kitty," I call, as I search for her with LuLu on my tail. I'd be better off leaving her be, so I won't sneeze so much.

"Keep her out of your bedroom," my doctor tells me as he prescribes pills, eye drops and nose spray for my allergic reaction.

"Okay," I say, as I stroke the outstretched cat lying next to me on my pillow.

I've learned that mothering and needing a mother is a universal instinct, whether human or animal, child or cat, mother or daughter.

SAVING FACE

Early on in our relationship, I had to get over the fact that my mother-in-law looked with disdain at my red-painted nails and glossy lipstick, so much so, I often felt like a harlot in her presence. The prospect of ever having plastic surgery would have banished me to hell altogether.

Driving with a friend to a luncheon some years ago, I marveled at how wonderful she looked after having had a face-lift a few days before. We sat side-by-side in her sports-car when I sensed her studying me at red lights. Upon our arrival, she pointed out all my facial flaws and suggested I have a face-lift right away before my down-turned jowls and sagging neck further deteriorated.

I dissolved into her bucket seat. Staring at the silver-staples sticking out of her scalp and still-fresh black and blues ringing her ears and eyes, I told her between clenched teeth, I was happy her surgical enhancement gave her a new feeling of confidence, but she'd best take her exuberance elsewhere. Then I got out of the car and slammed the door in her brand new face.

Six months later, she called to apologize—said her psychiatrist advised her to, apparently to absolve herself of the guilt she'd built up over her insensitive remarks. Again, it was all about preserving her. . . first her face, then her psyche.

A decade later we are no longer friends, but her attempt to tell me something I didn't want to hear continues to dog me. I think about it a lot these days, not necessarily in terms of my face, but in every way my body suddenly needs fixing, from my looks to my shape—my hair to my feet. Moving past menopause into middle-age, a transformation has stripped my dewy youth and replaced it with gray hair, brittle bones, dry skin and bent fingers.

All at once it seems, I'm faced with camouflaging the mini-breakdowns that are starting to make me feel like a used car with ever-increasing mileage, and I'm having to go into the shop more often for repairs.

What shop? For starters, it's the colorist at the hairdresser's to cover the roots and sideburns that stubbornly sprout their true, dull, silvery-gray hues every four weeks. Even my eyebrows have to be dyed once a month to keep up with the ruse.

My rough elbows and knees are so wrinkled they look like Chinese Shar Pei. Out of nowhere, brown patches appear on my arms and legs, skin-tags on my neck, liver spots and moles grow where I can't see but feel them and the dermatologist takes pictures of it all and asks "have you always had that?" What's really scary is the mind begins to go when you say you can't remember.

Decades of walking have formed thick padded soles on the bottom of my feet. I take them to the podiatrist, a place I remember my elderly grandmother used to go to for her insufferable and unsightly bunions. He clips nails that have turned yellow and hard—like my hair they too, have lost their luster—and shaves corns and calluses as if he's whittling wood. He tells me to wear sensible shoes with big boxy toes to take the pressure off my aging feet and never to wear high heels again. He's a man, I tell myself, and has no idea how cruel that prescription is.

Those sensible shoes have to be tied with fingers that swell with the changing seasons. My wedding band doesn't fit most summer days, and the hands to which they are attached have to be kept out of water to protect them from splitting open and, to prevent that, need to be slathered with unguent and covered with rubber gloves.

Hips like battle tanks flank the spreading armada of cellulite that invades my mid-section and conquers my waist. What used to be in the 20-inch range is now in the 30s and what was once in the 30s has moved up into the 40s. And on the scale — my normal weight is approaching what I once was when I was pregnant with twins.

What lies ahead is even more frightening. I recall my 90+ year old aunts with their concave stomachs and diminishing postures, curled-in and convex, as if folding back into the fetuses they once were. Bones, formerly unseen to the naked-eye, popped out of their anatomies and became prominent features in their spines, knees, necks and wrists. The tiny metacarpals in their fingers no longer followed one straight uninterrupted line but broke into different directions as if they'd earned retirement. That, plus the obvious need to wear bifocals and have cataract surgery, are all likely to be in my future too.

But what I see in the morning, every day, in the mirror, is my face. I wonder if the time has finally come for nips and tucks. I know I have options my aunts would never have considered, even had they been available in their heydays. I could botox my forehead, liposuct the chicken-fat in my neck, have collagen injected into the wrinkles around my mouth and eyes, and laser-zap one unsightly hair that keeps growing back on my chin.

That hair is genetic. My long-gone-grandmother had such a hair, though it never seemed to bother her. But then, she never had a friend with a sports-car who had a face-lift and went to the shrink.

DON'T CALL ME CARMELA

One thing my mother-in-law and I had in common was not knowing anyone who was in the Mafia.

A few months after we were married and my husband's career began to soar, Grandma Beatrice asked me if he was a mafioso. My insides crumbled. How could she think that? Pulling words from my dry throat, I explained it was my husband's education and skills in business that made him a success. She told me everyone she knew who had money was in some way connected to shady dealings.

The day after the season finale of HBO's wildly popular mobster drama, "The Sopranos," one of the porters in my New York City building greeted me with a big and loud, "Hey, here comes Mrs. Soprano!." It was as if he said "screw you fat lady." I opened my mouth to say something but my tongue turned to rubber. The doorman and other residents milling about the lobby waited in titillating silence for me to respond. Fumbling to grab hold of my falling packages, I finally regained my footing and my voice. "You have no idea how wrong you are!" I said, outraged at the slur.

More than insulted, I was hurt.

There's a common feeling among Italian Americans that others see us as a thin-skinned ethnic group, unable to poke fun at ourselves and quick to point out defamation when we sense we're being discriminated against. Not that I'm a prima donna, but I just don't view myself that way.

Like everyone else who jumped on the Soprano's bandwagon, I too looked forward to watching its ongoing Sunday night saga, not because it's about me or people I know — but quite the opposite. I'm just as curious as the next person to discover what the life of a powerful gun-toting mobster, his dysfunctional family and coterie of made-men are like.

I watched The Sopranos to be entertained just as I did The Godfather movies, getting as caught up as everyone else cheering Sonny Corleone on for beating up his brother-in-law out of respect for his sister. The Bronx Tale is one of my favorite movies, not because of cursing and shooting and wise-guy buffonery, but because of the moral lesson a hard-working bus-driver tries to teach his mob-idolizing son, that "it's better to be loved than feared."

If there were mobsters in the Bushwick neighborhood where I grew up, I never recognized one. The only shady dealings I heard discussed among the men-folk on Grove Street was playing the "numbers," whenever a new baby was born or when someone moved to a new address. Otherwise, there has never been a Big Pussy or Paulie Walnuts in my life.

So why do I look forward to watching shows these types of characters are in?

Because of everything good that rises above the sinister underworld. What I remember tenderly of Martin Scorsese's film "Goodfellas" is the meal his mother prepared for the character Joe Pesci played and his mobster buddies. She did so—unquestioningly, unconditionally, like most Italian mothers—unaware of what her son has done that day, which just happened to be hack a body to pieces and stuff it in the trunk of his car. That the son was at the mother's table was enough for her to be happy and in an uncanny way, it's her character that is innocent and endearing and like many women I know in real-life Italian American households.

Though, Tony Soprano's scheming mother Livia, didn't quite fall into this endearing category, other characters on the show do. They slap each other on the back, kiss and hug hello and goodbye, cry when they or their loved ones are hurting and are not afraid to be demonstrative—compassionate and gentle even—to those within their own wickedly depraved world.

When an elderly female neighbor tries to rekindle a long-lost relationship with Uncle Junior by cooking him a tray of homemade lasagne upon his return from a hospital stay, the feisty skirt-chasing tough-guy is touched by the gesture. His reaction is a familiar one. For Italians, food is the bonding force—the starchy fixative that brings the family—be it blood relations or a brotherhood sealed by blood oaths—together in a sacred rite. That most of the scenes shot in Tony Soprano's household take place in the kitchen, around the counter and sink where food is prepared and where the oft-opened refrigerator is practically a character itself, is not surprising.

From my own immigrant lineage I know how parents who never went to college want their children to do better, and as a parent myself, I can relate to the ups and downs of Tony and Carmela's emotions—their pride in daughter Meadow's ability to get into a good college, and aching concern over the young Anthony's aimless lethargy.

And the combat-like yet forgiving nature of Carmela, when she learns of her husband's "gooma" and his sexual attraction to the female analyst whose name he calls out in the middle of the night, is a gender-thing—a reaction all women can empathize with. Just as protecting her husband from their childrens' inquisitiveness about his "business-dealings" is a couple-thing—all parents at one time or another find themselves defending each other in the eyes of their children.

Under the circumstances, Carmela's seeking solace from a priest and flirting with the house-painter to fill the lonely hole her husband left in her heart could have conceivably been made by the love-starved wives of Irish Americans, Latin Americans or American Americans.

Living in a suburban home on the outskirts of a town that has a local sports' store, pork store, and an Italian restaurant owned by a friend, the Sopranos' lifestyle feels so familiar, so regular and normal, the setting represents how untold numbers of modern-day Italian Americans actually do live. It also reflects the nouveau-riche status of any ethnic group that's lifted itself to a higher rung on a class-based ladder with all of its clearly visible accoutrements: a big sprawling hilltop house, expensive cars, flashy jewelry and analysts on retainer.

All else does not. The image of smug cigar-chomping dons and capos who operate out of X-rated dance clubs to front for gambling, shake-downs, thefts, loan-sharking, break-ins, pay-offs, drug deals and hard, cold murder continues to be exploited via cinema, TV, novels and the news media, way out of proportion to the number of Italian-Americans actually involved in such depravity. Sadly, it is this characterization that remains imbedded — to the point of glorification — in America's psyche.

Never once did it occur to me that others would think that's who I am too.

Yet I continue to be a voyeuristic accomplice perpetuating the slim myth.

I, and, I suspect, other Italian-Americans like me, see what's not so obvious in the portrayals of these characters — eschewing the loud banging of the kettle drum, for the soft background music — the nostalgia for that which is familiar.

The scene that I can recite by heart from "Godfather I" is not the one in which Don Corleone promises his backroom cronies to "make offers that can't be refused," but the one in which his simple wife, the family's matriarch, Mama Corleone, sings along to an old Sicilian ditty at her daughter's wedding. Why? Because "C'è la luna a mezzo mare," was the very song I danced to, rocking in a slow lilting embrace, with my beloved Sicilian grandmother at my own wedding.

So, you can call me Mrs. Cuomo, Mrs. LaSorda, Mrs. Scalia; call me Mrs. Panetta, Mrs. Capra, but never call me Carmela. My husband is no Tony Soprano.

CRYSTAL BALL

Even when, in later years, she could afford to splurge on the finest cut of meat or freshly picked fruit, my mother-in-law was never able to break out of her frugal background. It was her nature to pick through the worst of the lot at half-priced bargain counters and spin it into gold.

Playing a fortune-teller's game with a piece of composition paper, its four corners folded points inward and again in eighths on the opposite side, we preteen girls placed our fingers beneath all four corners and worked them in and out to discover what our futures held. Each taking our turns, we watched with great glee as categories were spelled out and, when uncovered, revealed where we would live, what kind of car we'd drive, whether we'd be rich or famous, whom we would marry and how many children we'd have.

Players listed four hoped-for possibilities in each category. The most popular choices for houses were mansion, beach-house, ski chalet and penthouse. Cars fell into two favored groups: hotrods like the Corvette, MG and GTO, and the luxuries — Cadillac and limo, but occasionally a beach buggy or Volkswagen Beetle surfaced too. The most titillating picks involved prospective mates, which were the hardest choices to make because many of us set our sights on the same handsome boy, and we were not necessarily eager to let each other know about it. It was especially hard for me, a pre-pubescent roly-poly up against the all-American cheerleader types who everyone already knew would wind up with the most popular guys anyway.

But even I could dream. So I went about choosing my roster of eligible boys; which Beatle I wanted to go out on a date with — my favorite was Ringo — and whether I'd become a movie star, singer, Miss America or Playboy Bunny.

As the future emerged, it turned out I got my handsome man, a 10-room mansion, my hot-rod — a Jeep Cherokee — but never did have the 6 or 9 kids I thought I'd pop out one after the other to form either a basketball or baseball team. I only had three, but the two that came first, in a burst of unexpected twins, kind of put the kabosh on my long-held fantasy of becoming the old woman in the shoe who with so many children, she didn't know what to do.

I did know what to do — at least at first.

At 24 I married a man who was educated but not quite settled in his life's work. I'd been the chief breadwinner back then, managing to save up $6000 teaching elementary school while he studied economics in graduate school. My entire savings were eventually spent on a less-than-a-carat diamond engagement ring and a blow-out wedding reception for 200 people at the Astorian Manor replete with Viennese Table and Buster Long's symphonic eight-piece orchestra.

"Le buste," the wedding envelopes filled with mostly $25-a-couple fell short of our per $30 per-couple outlay for the reception, so recouping the money we initially invested in the affair didn't materialize as planned. By the time we returned from our honeymoon and bought some furniture for our tiny Bronx apartment, the newly opened joint bank account under Mr. & Mrs. had dwindled precipitously to $200. We fell deeper into a financial hole three months into our marriage when I returned home from work one day to discover the door ajar and our apartment ransacked. Gone were a borrowed TV which we had to make good for, all of our liquor and every last piece of my new husband's clothing.

Just before the wedding, my spouse-to-be's first attempt to get full-time job was with an insurance agency less than a mile away from the Fordham neighborhood where he'd grown up. His mother was thrilled, we'd already rented an apartment a mile away from her in one of the two-family homes off Pelham Parkway, so if her son worked close-by too, all the better. But that didn't happen. When he turned down the meager-paying sales position to wait for a better offer, his mother went after him like a honking goose. And when a better offer finally did materialize to get in on a ground-floor position in an old established marine shipping firm in Manhattan, it was even more of a heartbreak for my new mother-in-law because her son's lofty pursuit of a Ph.D. stopped dramatically short. Though he completed his course work and exams, a new job and new marriage consumed too much of his unbound energy for him to research and write a thesis.

That my mother-in-law considered this one of the greatest failures of her life—because her older son obtained a doctorate in English at the age of 23—was evident in her constant reminder that marriage had gotten in the way of the dynasty of family PhD's she was trying to build. While her constant badgering to go back to school rolled off my young husband's back like rain on a slicker, it stuck to me like wet underwear.

Things got worse before they got better. I was 7 months pregnant when our landlord put the two-family house we were living in up for sale. Left with little choice but to move, and given the critical timing of my impending birth, my young husband decided the best thing to do would be to buy the house ourselves. Problem was, we didn't have a single cent of its $45,000 price tag. He pleaded with his mother for a loan for the down payment—it was she, not the men in her 3-person household who controlled the family bank-book—the powerful matriarch balked, and barked, finding yet another reason to scold my husband for not finishing his PhD—but her youngest offspring was equally willful and, before long, they were walking arm-in-arm to the bank.

Buying the house proved to be a serendipitous decision on my husband's part, for less than a month later, not one, but two babies arrived five weeks before their due date, and we at least didn't have to worry about where we were going to put them.

Six and a half weeks later when the premies both managed to gain enough weight to be released from Jacobi Hospital, we took them home, but not without a head-to-head battle with administrators over the bill. They fully expected us to pay the $30,000 for critical care our children received, because our health insurance only covered normal births. When we told the very important men sitting behind the very big desk we couldn't possibly pay that amount, they asked if we owned a house. Both of us fell painfully silent. Eventually my young husband worked out a deal to pay the hospital $25 a week and we took our new babies home to our new house.

It would have taken over twenty years to eliminate that debt, and 15 years to pay off our mortgage, and we still had my mother-in-law's loan, but all were paid off well in advance as a result of my husband's changing jobs, and with it, our lives changed exponentially.

He worked hard as a ship-broker, burning candles at both ends of the day, traveled around the world and fed off of growing successes. On the home-front, I mothered as he labored and we quickly began to outgrow our space and place.

Whereas he thought in grand swathes of limitless borders — wanting to invest in high-end property that would appreciate with time — I thought in reverse, desiring a more secure picket fence, with neighbors next door. We settled on a combination of both in what, given our backgrounds, was indeed a mansion — a 5 bedroom split-ranch on Long Island with a two car garage on a corner lot, a block from Manhasset Bay in a neighborhood with lots of basketball hoops.

It was thrilling to move for the first time ever out of our Brooklyn and Bronx locales, but it was equally as scary to step into the land of Oz. The first thing I noticed was my clothes weren't right. I needed to build a more sophisticated wardrobe — had to change from sneakers to shoes, boots even; carry real leather handbags, look for clothes with recognizable labels and wear lots of scarves. There were so many things I was never exposed to — nursery schools and private country clubs, community fairs and church socials, fashion shows, progressive dinners and charity luncheons where I learned the traits of bidding, donating and volunteering.

We bought our luxury car—a Cadillac, hired a lawn service and installed a burglar alarm so we'd never have to worry about being robbed again. I began to arrange sit-down dinners for my husband's growing cadre of business associates, serving them a more gourmet fare than I'd been used to on fine china with folded cloth napkins and crystal goblets More and more I found the need for weekly manicures and more frequent trips to the hairstylist, at quintuple the cost of what I'd paid in the Bronx. I organized play-dates for the children and met with other mothers at the park, the pool, tennis courts, skating rink, duck pond and for story-time at the local library.

And like those other young mothers newly planted in the land of milk and honey, I too began to blossom with a second pregnancy and a long-awaited third (and hoped for, single) child.

By the time she arrived on the scene, my husband's business was flourishing and our five member household had risen into the rarified strata in which more than half of our income was paid to the government.

"I didn't know we were rich," my youngest daughter exclaimed when we sold the Manhasset house we'd lived in for 20 years and moved into an 8 room condo in the heart of Manhattan's upper east side. She said it as if it were a bad thing.

Knowing full well that we were hardly on a par with the Vanderbilts and Rockefellers of the world, I apologized. "Maybe we are, but what does being rich mean?"

I know a long time ago it meant owning a mansion, marrying a successful and handsome man and driving a fancy new car. If our present life meets that criteria, then I guess we are. But I don't feel rich, I feel guilty because my dream has been realized while most others' haven't and I'm afraid they no longer view me as an equal. My husband suffers from a different kind of guilt. Through all that he's achieved, he still feels a sense of loss for not writing his thesis and pursuing his PhD so many years ago. Which goes to show that being rich doesn't necessarily equate with being successful, especially when it's viewed through the eyes of one's mother. Even if she's no longer of this world.

MAMMA MIA, MARIA

I felt triumphant the summer day so long ago when my future husband finally decided it was time to bring me home to meet his mother. Stepping into the six room first-floor corner apartment on 188th Street and Lorillard Place in the Fordham section of the Bronx, I felt as though I'd arrived at destiny's door. There was no question in my mind I'd pass the toughest scrutiny with flying colors since all my friends viewed me as an old-fashioned Italian girl, the kind any young fellow would like to bring home to his mamma, so I was confident that this particular Italian mamma would find me suitable for her son.

I must have been dreaming. That, or I had no idea what real Italian mothers were like—the kind who sailed to America but left their hearts and minds and visions of future grandchildren heavily anchored in the old country.

Led through a long dark hallway into the kitchen, what I first noticed about Mike's Mamma Maria, was how attached to the sink she was. She didn't budge when she saw me; instead, I had to walk over and greet her, near the sink where she was busily preparing some type of food... if you could call cow's brains food. My throat still tightens at the thought of the grayish gelatinous mass that was being scrambled into an omelet for the afternoon meal, an event of primary importance in Mamma Maria's household, I quickly noted. The young Siciliana her baby boy sprung on her at lunchtime without fair warning that fateful day was secondary.

But then I soon learned, so was everything else in Mamma Maria's world. With the exception of her compliant husband and two devoted sons what really mattered were concrete things that she could take charge of, like the bed, which was made in a flurry the minute my father-in-law lifted his head off the pillow—and the floor, swept repeatedly with a witch-like broom that stood against the living room wall as if it were a piece of furniture itself, and of course the timeworn sink where lamb's heads and elbows, underwear and broccoli di rape were all scrubbed and drubbed with the same thorough intensity.

This was my mother-in-law's little bit of territory, her patch of feudal land, and she ruled it with such passion, even the fibers in the couch stood at attention when she entered the room. Eeking her way through the depression and two world wars as a single parent in the land of "miseria" no doubt, taught her survival skills she adapted to everyday life. Yet, even after she arrived in the land of throw-aways she continued to make everything with her own two gnarled and reliable hands—clothes, anisette, delicately crocheted tablecloths and coarsely knitted shawls. Nothing was wasted. If a knitted blanket unraveled, it became two sweaters. What was used to the point of abuse and fell apart, was then used again for something else: old shirts became clothespin bags, chicken bones flavored the next day's soup, orange peels were saved and resurfaced in biscotti—even wet coffee grinds were dumped as a natural fertilizer around the roots of her brother's prized fig tree. The hardest thing for "Mamma Maria" to do was to throw something away.

Gently soiled napkins were reused, wet paper towels were hung out to dry; dead leaves served as mulch for next season's tomato plants, and cherished photographs were framed with a border of crinkled tinfoil and hung with string. Money was never wasted on clothes sent to the dry-cleaner, instead suit pants and jackets were draped across the clothesline and beaten with a long wooden paddle. This ancient ritual caused Mike to sneak the few good pieces of clothing he'd bought at the upscale B & G Men's Shop on

187th Street, with money he'd earned at odd jobs, to the tailor's and back. He'd hear about it for a month if he was caught.

Because according to "Mamma Maria," only those things made in Italy were valued, everything made elsewhere, especially n'America, was "fatta male" of poor quality. The four good dresses that hung in her closet for over fifty years, one heavy coat restyled from my father-in-law's military issue, and half a dozen aprons with threaded needles permanently pinned to their bosoms were all made with material that came with her from Italy, as did the few pieces of thin, almost-bendable, 18 carat gold jewelry she wore around her neck, on her fingers, and dangling conservatively from her ears.

But those weren't her real jewels, besides her children, her most prized possessions were venerated statues of the Blessed Mother, St. Frances of Assisi, St. Anthony and Padre Pio; crucifixes adorned with rosary beads and honored with votive candles and plastic flowers, and the mismatched sets of cracked dishes and cups and thin enameled pots she equally revered.

"Mamma Maria" had an aversion to excess except when it came to food. Along with the stalwartness of her deep, tub-like sink, the triangle of my mother-in-law's daily life was set into predictable motion between two other points in her kitchen: her trusty stove, scarred with decades of boiling and frothy spillovers; and her battle weary refrigerator, where limp bunches of escarole hung haphazardly over open containers of ricotta cheese and pickled eggplant.

From the time she rose until she went to sleep, my mother-in-law's day was regimented around the noontime meal. My father-in-law's night-time job as an elevator operator at the U.S. Post Office on 33rd Street in Manhattan, and my brother-in-law's flexible schedule teaching classes at the university, made that possible, much to Mike's frustration.

Growing up an American boy, a baby-boomer, living in a household that was decidedly run in a different time and place, he cringed with embarrassment, he told me candidly, whenever she called out the window to the schoolyard across the street, "Maichine" (little Michael) e ora di mangiare (it's time for lunch), stopping all action in the middle of a rough and tumble football game or when all neighborhood bets were riding on "Mikey Heart" to pitch a winning baseball game.

Home was all "Mamma Maria" knew. She never went out to restaurants, movies or amusements of any sort because she didn't trust what was being served or understand what was being said. When she did go out, it was within the safe confines of her tightly knit ethnic neighborhood: on daily forays to the enclosed Arthur Avenue "marketa" or to Mt. Carmel Church where she attended the daily Italian language mass (making novenas every time there was a new reason to peitition her "Gesu") and for the annual feasts held twice a year just two blocks from her home. The only other time she'd step out of her cloistered environs, put on one of her four good dresses and military-strength coat was to attend literary functions involving my brother-in-law whose lofty accomplishments as a "professore di letturatura italiana" were a great source of maternal pride and joy.

I was but a fly on her screen, but she loomed as large as Arnold Schwarzenegger on mine. Her earthiness constantly startled me. She was fearless—like the time she put her knitting down, went over to the TV, violently slapped a huge bug crawling up the side of it with her bare hands and quietly returned to her knitting. Or when she cut the bad part off a banana or melon, or the green mold off a chunk of provolone and instructed me to eat the rest—"mangia, è buona," Dutifully, I obeyed, the food sliding down my throat in dripping mouthfuls, never once complaining for the lack of crunch.

There was no guilt in her actions, because everything was done with the best intentions and anyone attempting to argue otherwise would be reminded of that. "Mamma Maria" was determined to get her way, and to my profound amazement no one tried to stop her. She was the winner of all battles, confident and smart, particularly at "la marketa" where the merchants stood at attention like the fibers on her couch, when she walked up to their stalls, examined their produce, and bargained for lower and lower prices until, in a true test of her mighty will, they dropped to their knees and gave the zucchini and prezzemolo (parsley) to her out of mercy.

She didn't look the way she acted. On first glance, her tiny 5 foot frame made her seem fragile but one would have had to bake bread with her to know what she was capable of. She used men's Vaseline Hair Oil to style her hair and it was never out of place. She didn't own a toothbrush, but instead used salt on her index finger and scrubbed her teeth vigorously, which worked well enough since she had all her own teeth for 95 years. She never wore make-up or nail polish during her lifetime, and left a note in her will instructing her sons to honor her wish to remain in her natural state when she died. Her four good dresses were all in dark colors, her shoes and purse never anything but black since she always seemed to be in a perpetual state of mourning for someone she knew.

Those somber colors made her skin more noticeable — her square-set face was a striking contrast of translucence, in pinky-white — many shades lighter than mine. Her legs too, were thin all the way up and could very well have graced the stage at Radio City, but unfortunately no one ever saw them — except me when she raised her dress at times to show me things that could only be delicately discussed among women.

She'd give you the apron off her chest if she loved you. My children and I were the recipients of that. We were always welcome at her dinner table and able to call upon her at a moment's notice to babysit or repair a ripped garment. She never turned us down for anything as long as she felt it was safe, decent and healthy within her own highly held standards.

Every gift I ever gave her was never used. I tried to make things easier in small increments by buying her new pots for Christmas, a new bathrobe for her birthday, a bedspread, brightly colored sweater, new dresses, gloves . . . even a broom with all its bristles intact, but they were all relegated to a closet where they were neatly stored away.

"Questa è per te quando io morrò," this is for you when I die, she said. I was beaten down, it was futile to try to change her, please her, and always felt as if I was at the short end of a perpetual tug-of-war. Sometimes I cried, though not in front of her. I wanted so much to make a contribution to her life—to make her see there was an easier way, but she was not about to take lessons from, "una giovane" the young one.

This indomitable woman was naturally suspect of new things because they didn't stand the test of time—hadn't proved their worth, and held no place among her rarified artifacts. "Mamma Mia" only accepted that which was familiar into her circle of beings and belongings, and somehow, after 30 years, miraculously I'd become one of them.

Did I say "Mamma Mia?"

EPILOGUE

December 5, 1989

Dear Sons,

    Let me tell you these few words. As soon as The Lord wants me, I embrace Him with all my heart. Don't cry! I will always be present amongst you and I will pray for you. May the Lord grant me a full eternity to pray for all of you.

    Joseph, let me remind you of what I have always told you — when I die, I want only my eyes and mouth closed. No lipstick, no rouge, no cotton in my cheeks. I want to remain as I have always lived all of my life, just as The Lord has created and redeemed me.

    One more thing: put in my casket my brother's letters, which my mother wanted. I will bring them to her. I want to stay only one evening in the funeral parlor so that I may be taken soon to the house of my Heavenly rest.

    I embrace you all,

Your Mamma.

P.S. Please, please read this letter and listen to me. If you don't do as I say, I'll be disappointed.

POSTSCRIPT

Maria Tusiani left this world three hours short of her 95th birthday ... or, so we thought. My son-in-law reminded us the six hour time difference in her Italian homeland, allowed her to reach that lofty milestone after all.

What she never lived to see —

Her younger son was finally awarded an honorary doctorate degree.

Her older son moved out of the Bronx and is living a bachelor's life in Manhattan.

Her eldest granddaughter married a man from the Italian province of Shanghai!

VIA Folios

A refereed book series dedicated to the culture of Italians and Italian Americans.

MARIA GIURA. *What My Father Taught Me*. Vol. 127. Poetry.
STANISLAO PUGLIESE. *A Century of Sinatra*. Vol. 126. Popular Culture. $12
TONY ARDIZZONE. *The Arab's Ox*. Vol. 125. Novel. $18
PHYLLIS CAPELLO. *Packs Small Plays Big*. Vol. 124. Poetry.
FRED GARDAPHÉ. *Read 'em and Reap*. Vol. 123. Criticism. $22
JOSEPH A. AMATO. *Diagnostics*. Vol 122. Literature. $12.
DENNIS BARONE. *Second Thoughts*. Vol 121. Poetry. $10
OLIVIA K. CERRONE. *The Hunger Saint*. Vol 120. Novella. $12
GARIBLADI M. LAPOLLA. *Miss Rollins in Love*. Vol 119. Novel. $24
JOSEPH TUSIANI. *A Clarion Call*. Vol 118. Poetry. $16
JOSEPH A. AMATO. *My Three Sicilies*. Vol 117. Poetry & Prose. $17
MARGHERITA COSTA. *Voice of a Virtuosa and Coutesan*. Vol 116. Poetry. $24
NICOLE SANTALUCIA. *Because I Did Not Die*. Vol 115. Poetry. $12
MARK CIABATTARI. *Preludes to History*. Vol 114. Poetry. $12
HELEN BAROLINI. *Visits*. Vol 113. Novel. $22
ERNESTO LIVORNI. *The Fathers' America*. Vol. 112. Poetry. $14
MARIO B. MIGNONE. *The Story of My People*. Vol 111. Non-fiction. $17
GEORGE GUIDA. *The Sleeping Gulf*. Vol 110. Poetry. $14
JOEY NICOLETTI. *Reverse Graffiti*. Vol 109. Poetry. $14
GIOSE RIMANELLI. *Il mestiere del furbo*. Vol 108. Criticism. $20
LEWIS TURCO. *The Hero Enkidu*. Vol 107. Poetry. $14
AL TACCONELLI. *Perhaps Fly*. Vol. 106. Poetry. $14
RACHEL GUIDO DEVRIES. *A Woman Unknown in Her Bones*. Vol 105. Poetry. $11
BERNARD BRUNO. *A Tear and a Tear in My Heart*. Vol. 104. Non-fiction. $20
FELIX STEFANILE. *Songs of the Sparrow*. Vol. 103. Poetry. $30
FRANK POLIZZI. *A New Life with Bianca*. Vol 102. Poetry. $10
GIL FAGIANI. *Stone Walls*. Vol 101. Poetry. $14
LOUISE DESALVO. *Casting Off*. Vol 100. Fiction. $22
MARY JO BONA. *I Stop Waiting for You*. Vol. 99. Poetry. $12
RACHEL GUIDO DEVRIES. *Stati zitt, Josie*. Vol 98. Children's Literature. $8
GRACE CAVALIERI. *The Mandate of Heaven*. Vol 97. Poetry. $14
MARISA FRASCA. *Via incanto*. Vol 96. Poetry. $12
DOUGLAS GLADSTONE. *Carving a Niche for Himself*. Vol 95. History. $12
MARIA TERRONE. *Eye to Eye*. Vol 94. Poetry. $14
CONSTANCE SANCETTA. *Here in Cerchio*. Vol 93. Local History. $15

MARIA MAZZIOTTI GILLAN. *Ancestors' Song.* Vol 92. Poetry. $14
MICHAEL PARENTI. *Waiting for Yesterday: Pages from a Street Kid's Life.* Vol 90. Memoir. $15
ANNIE LANZILOTTO. *Schistsong.* Vol 89. Poetry. $15
EMANUEL DI PASQUALE. *Love Lines.* Vol 88. Poetry. $10
CAROSONE & LOGIUDICE. *Our Naked Lives.* Vol 87. Essays. $15
JAMES PERICONI. *Strangers in a Strange Land: A Survey of Italian-Language American Books.*Vol 86. Book History. $24
DANIELA GIOSEFFI. *Escaping La Vita Della Cucina.* Vol 85. Essays. $22
MARIA FAMÀ. *Mystics in the Family.* Vol 84. Poetry. $10
ROSSANA DEL ZIO. *From Bread and Tomatoes to Zuppa di Pesce "Ciambotto".*Vol. 83. $15
LORENZO DELBOCA. *Polentoni.* Vol 82. Italian Studies. $15
SAMUEL GHELLI. *A Reference Grammar.* Vol 81. Italian Language. $36
ROSS TALARICO. *Sled Run.* Vol 80. Fiction. $15
FRED MISURELLA. *Only Sons.* Vol 79. Fiction. $14
FRANK LENTRICCHIA. *The Portable Lentricchia.* Vol 78. Fiction. $16
RICHARD VETERE. *The Other Colors in a Snow Storm.* Vol 77. Poetry. $10
GARIBALDI LAPOLLA. *Fire in the Flesh.* Vol 76 Fiction & Criticism. $25
GEORGE GUIDA. *The Pope Stories.* Vol 75 Prose. $15
ROBERT VISCUSI. *Ellis Island.* Vol 74. Poetry. $28
ELENA GIANINI BELOTTI. *The Bitter Taste of Strangers Bread.* Vol 73. Fiction. $24
PINO APRILE. *Terroni.* Vol 72. Italian Studies. $20
EMANUEL DI PASQUALE. *Harvest.* Vol 71. Poetry. $10
ROBERT ZWEIG. *Return to Naples.* Vol 70. Memoir. $16
AIROS & CAPPELLI. *Guido.* Vol 69. Italian/American Studies. $12
FRED GARDAPHÉ. *Moustache Pete is Dead! Long Live Moustache Pete!.* Vol 67. Literature/Oral History. $12
PAOLO RUFFILLI. *Dark Room/Camera oscura.* Vol 66. Poetry. $11
HELEN BAROLINI. *Crossing the Alps.* Vol 65. Fiction. $14
COSMO FERRARA. *Profiles of Italian Americans.* Vol 64. Italian Americana. $16
GIL FAGIANI. *Chianti in Connecticut.* Vol 63. Poetry. $10
BASSETTI & D'ACQUINO. *Italic Lessons.* Vol 62. Italian/American Studies. $10
CAVALIERI & PASCARELLI, Eds. *The Poet's Cookbook.* Vol 61. Poetry/Recipes. $12
EMANUEL DI PASQUALE. *Siciliana.* Vol 60. Poetry. $8
NATALIA COSTA, Ed. *Bufalini.* Vol 59. Poetry. $18.
RICHARD VETERE. *Baroque.* Vol 58. Fiction. $18.
LEWIS TURCO. *La Famiglia/The Family.* Vol 57. Memoir. $15
NICK JAMES MILETI. *The Unscrupulous.* Vol 56. Humanities. $20
BASSETTI. ACCOLLA. D'AQUINO. *Italici: An Encounter with Piero Bassetti.* Vol 55. Italian Studies. $8

GIOSE RIMANELLI. *The Three-legged One*. Vol 54. Fiction. $15
CHARLES KLOPP. *Bele Antiche Stòrie*. Vol 53. Criticism. $25
JOSEPH RICAPITO. *Second Wave*. Vol 52. Poetry. $12
GARY MORMINO. *Italians in Florida*. Vol 51. History. $15
GIANFRANCO ANGELUCCI. *Federico F*. Vol 50. Fiction. $15
ANTHONY VALERIO. *The Little Sailor*. Vol 49. Memoir. $9
ROSS TALARICO. *The Reptilian Interludes*. Vol 48. Poetry. $15
RACHEL GUIDO DE VRIES. *Teeny Tiny Tino's Fishing Story*. Vol 47. Children's Literature. $6
EMANUEL DI PASQUALE. *Writing Anew*. Vol 46. Poetry. $15
MARIA FAMÀ. *Looking For Cover*. Vol 45. Poetry. $12
ANTHONY VALERIO. *Toni Cade Bambara's One Sicilian Night*. Vol 44. Poetry. $10
EMANUEL CARNEVALI. *Furnished Rooms*. Vol 43. Poetry. $14
BRENT ADKINS. et al., Ed. *Shifting Borders. Negotiating Places*. Vol 42. Conference. $18
GEORGE GUIDA. *Low Italian*. Vol 41. Poetry. $11
GARDAPHÈ, GIORDANO, TAMBURRI. *Introducing Italian Americana*. Vol 40. Italian/American Studies. $10
DANIELA GIOSEFFI. *Blood Autumn/Autunno di sangue*. Vol 39. Poetry. $15/$25
FRED MISURELLA. *Lies to Live By*. Vol 38. Stories. $15
STEVEN BELLUSCIO. *Constructing a Bibliography*. Vol 37. Italian Americana. $15
ANTHONY JULIAN TAMBURRI, Ed. *Italian Cultural Studies 2002*. Vol 36. Essays. $18
BEA TUSIANI. *con amore*. Vol 35. Memoir. $19
FLAVIA BRIZIO-SKOV, Ed. *Reconstructing Societies in the Aftermath of War*. Vol 34. History. $30
TAMBURRI. et al., Eds. *Italian Cultural Studies 2001*. Vol 33. Essays. $18
ELIZABETH G. MESSINA, Ed. *In Our Own Voices*. Vol 32. Italian/American Studies. $25
STANISLAO G. PUGLIESE. *Desperate Inscriptions*. Vol 31. History. $12
HOSTERT & TAMBURRI, Eds. *Screening Ethnicity*. Vol 30. Italian/American Culture. $25
G. PARATI & B. LAWTON, Eds. *Italian Cultural Studies*. Vol 29. Essays. $18
HELEN BAROLINI. *More Italian Hours*. Vol 28. Fiction. $16
FRANCO NASI, Ed. *Intorno alla Via Emilia*. Vol 27. Culture. $16
ARTHUR L. CLEMENTS. *The Book of Madness & Love*. Vol 26. Poetry. $10
JOHN CASEY, et al. *Imagining Humanity*. Vol 25. Interdisciplinary Studies. $18
ROBERT LIMA. *Sardinia/Sardegna*. Vol 24. Poetry. $10
DANIELA GIOSEFFI. *Going On*. Vol 23. Poetry. $10
ROSS TALARICO. *The Journey Home*. Vol 22. Poetry. $12
EMANUEL DI PASQUALE. *The Silver Lake Love Poems*. Vol 21. Poetry. $7

JOSEPH TUSIANI. *Ethnicity*. Vol 20. Poetry. $12

JENNIFER LAGIER. *Second Class Citizen*. Vol 19. Poetry. $8

FELIX STEFANILE. *The Country of Absence*. Vol 18. Poetry. $9

PHILIP CANNISTRARO. *Blackshirts*. Vol 17. History. $12

LUIGI RUSTICHELLI, Ed. *Seminario sul racconto*. Vol 16. Narrative. $10

LEWIS TURCO. *Shaking the Family Tree*. Vol 15. Memoirs. $9

LUIGI RUSTICHELLI, Ed. *Seminario sulla drammaturgia*. Vol 14. Theater/Essays. $10

FRED GARDAPHÈ. *Moustache Pete is Dead! Long Live Moustache Pete!*. Vol 13. Oral Literature. $10

JONE GAILLARD CORSI. *Il libretto d'autore. 1860–1930*. Vol 12. Criticism. $17

HELEN BAROLINI. *Chiaroscuro: Essays of Identity*. Vol 11. Essays. $15

PICARAZZI & FEINSTEIN, Eds. *An African Harlequin in Milan*. Vol 10. Theater/Essays. $15

JOSEPH RICAPITO. *Florentine Streets & Other Poems*. Vol 9. Poetry. $9

FRED MISURELLA. *Short Time*. Vol 8. Novella. $7

NED CONDINI. *Quartettsatz*. Vol 7. Poetry. $7

ANTHONY JULIAN TAMBURRI, Ed. *Fuori: Essays by Italian/American Lesbiansand Gays*. Vol 6. Essays. $10

ANTONIO GRAMSCI. P. Verdicchio. Trans. & Intro. *The Southern Question*. Vol 5. Social Criticism. $5

DANIELA GIOSEFFI. *Word Wounds & Water Flowers*. Vol 4. Poetry. $8

WILEY FEINSTEIN. *Humility's Deceit: Calvino Reading Ariosto Reading Calvino*. Vol 3. Criticism. $10

PAOLO A. GIORDANO, Ed. *Joseph Tusiani: Poet. Translator. Humanist*. Vol 2. Criticism. $25

ROBERT VISCUSI. *Oration Upon the Most Recent Death of Christopher Columbus*. Vol 1. Poetry.

www.ingramcontent.com/pod-product-compliance
Lightning Source LLC
Chambersburg PA
CBHW022102090426
42743CB00008B/691